London's burning

D0800880

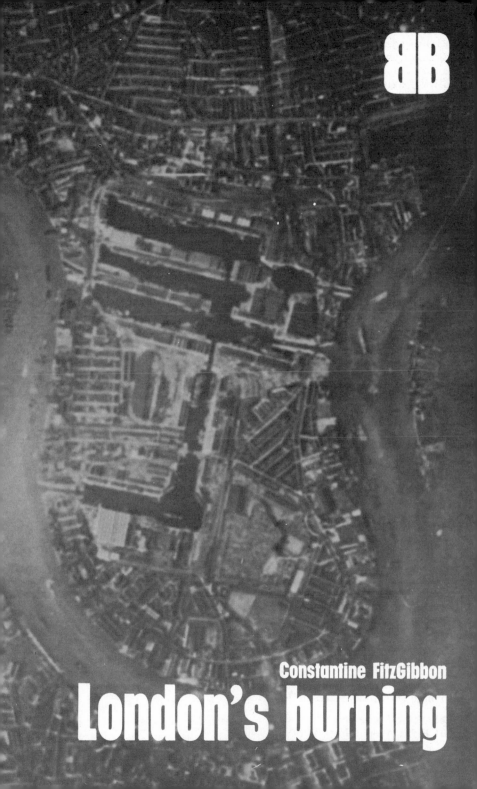

BB

Constantine FitzGibbon
London's burning

Editor-in-Chief: Barrie Pitt
Art Director: Peter Dunbar
Military Consultant: Sir Basil Liddell Hart
Picture Editor: Bobby Hunt
Editor: David Mason
Design: Sarah Kingham
Special Drawings: John Batchelor
Cartographer: Richard Natkiel
Cover: Denis Piper
Photographic Research: Nan Shuttleworth

Photographs for this book were specially selected from the following archives:
from left to right pages 2–3 Sado Opera Mundi; 6–7 Keystone; 9–10 Radio Times Hulton; 11 Black
Star; 12–14 Radio Times Hulton; 16 Keystone; 17 Radio Times Hulton; 18 Paul Popper Ltd/Radio
Times Hulton; 19 Radio Times Hulton; 20 Associated Press; 22 24 Imperial War Museum; 28–29
Suddeutscher Verlag; 30–33 IWM; 34–35 Keystone; 36–38 IWM; 40–41 United Press International; 44
IWM/Radio Times Hulton; 45–49 IWM; 51 AP; 52–53 IWM; 54 Sudd Verlag; 57–58 Keystone; 62 IWM;
63 Ullstein; 64 AP; 65 Black Star; 68–72 IWM; 74–75 Paul Popper Ltd; 77 AP/IWM; 78 IWM; 81 AP; 82–83
Paul Popper Ltd; 88 Radio Times Hulton; 92–93 AP; 95 IWM; 96–103 Keystone; 104 Ullstein; 108 Radio
Times Hulton; 112 Keystone; 115 IWM; 120–121 Black Star; 124–125 Heinrich Hoffman; 130 IWM;
132–133 Keystone; 135 Sado Opera Mundi; 136–137 Keystone; 140–141 IWM; 144 Radio Times Hulton;
146–148 IWM; 150–151 Keystone; 152–153 Radio Times Hulton; 154 IWM; 156–157 IWM
Front cover: IWM   Back cover: IWM

First printing: November 1970
Printed in United States of America

Ballantine Books Inc.
101 Fifth Avenue New York NY 10003

An Intext Publisher

Contents

The Blitz

Introduction by Barrie Pitt

By mid-July, 1940, the whole world knew that Britain faced attack, primarily from the air, on a scale hitherto unimagined outside the realms of horror-fiction or, significantly, outside the dry pedantism of official statistical forecasts of bombing potentialities. In Britain herself, the populace sustained their always phlegmatic attitude to possible calamity with the unreasonable but effective dogmas that as we now had no allies to support we also had none to let us down; and that as we had never been successfully invaded or defeated before, there was little likelihood of it happening now. There are circumstances in which there is much to be said for historical ignorance.

Being possessed, however, by a strong sense of national self-righteousness, we would have been somewhat disconcerted had we realised the cool objectivity with which the rest of the world regarded our plight, for although there were undoubtedly many individuals in Europe, in the Americas and of course, in the Commonwealth, who sympathised and were even genuinely alarmed at our situation, the majority of the populations of both North and South America, of Africa and of Asia, were either totally uninterested or unaware – and quite often of the opinion that it was time the stiff-necked islanders took a little beating. In the event, it was the population of London which took most of the beating, but in doing so they not only revealed to themselves that they were as good as their fathers had been (a useful reassurance at the beginning of what proved to be a long war) but won an astonishing amount of sympathy and indeed, admiration, from those beyond our shores who had watched the conflict. 'London can take it!' had been a slogan coined during the days immediately following the first onslaught, and she did indeed for many violent and scarifying weeks.

At first it was the East End which suffered – Poplar, Stepney, West Ham, Bermondsey and Rotherhithe – especially the rows of little, mean, back-to-back two storey cottages, built as cheaply and as quickly as the speculative builders of the 19th century

could put them up, and coiled closely through the dock areas; but then the bombers ranged further afield and Tottenham and Croydon, Chelsea and Trafalgar Square caught it, and then at the end of the year came the great fire raid on the City of London itself through which, as though by a miracle, St Paul's Cathedral stood virtually unscathed.

By the end of the year, London had excited the same world sympathy (even some, be it said, from among the ranks of her enemy) that had previously been accorded to Guernica, Warsaw and Rotterdam, and won additional respect as it became evident that none of the punishment taken had affected by one iota the national determination to withstand aggression until either it abated, or succeeded by annihilation. Thus London's fortitude reaped two harvests; it irritated Hitler to the extent that he eventually turned his back in disgust upon the stubborn islanders and directed his attentions eastwards towards the Russian plains where his armies were to be destroyed – and it won sympathy

and a great deal of material support from hitherto uncommitted nations and individuals.

We are fortunate that through it all, Constantine FitzGibbon was present to observe, to record and then to describe. Although even before it began, he had had the political insight and knowledge to perceive where ultimate good and evil lay and had acted upon his conclusions by enlisting in the Brigade of Guards, Mr. Fitz Gibbon is in fact an Irish American with opinions which contain little admiration for British attitudes, qualities or way of life. His account of the holocaust through which London passed, therefore, together with his analysis of the strategic and tactical reasons for its course and eventual climax, is objective and unmarred by excessive admiration for the people of whom he writes. But it is also – as readers of his other books will expect – superbly evocative, beautifully written, and alive with the compassion and creativity of the true artist.

Before the Blitz

The 7th September, 1940, was a Saturday. On that Saturday, a warm and sunny day, there occurred an event which had been dreaded for years, expected for over twelve months, and which now had been awaited with mounting certainty throughout that hot summer of battle, and defeat, and death. On 7th September, 1940, the German Air Force set out to destroy London.

Before describing the events of that day, and of the ensuing fifty-seven nights, when London was bombed each night and often by day as well, and of the six months that followed these, when London continued to be bombed frequently and heavily, it is as well to examine, quite briefly, the emotional, political and military background to the terrible winter that London was about to endure.

The aeroplane was first envisaged, from a military point of view, as an aid to reconnaissance. In August of 1914 the pilots of such planes, when they met, would shoot at one another with revolvers; such was the genesis of the fighter plane. Later they also carried grenades, which they dropped on the enemy's trenches, and the bomber was born. The first bomb to be dropped by a German aeroplane on British soil – or indeed by any warplane on a target that was not directly connected with a battlefield – fell near Dover Castle, on 24th December, 1914, and broke a number of panes of glass. The bombing of London, however, which began in 1915, was for the first two years by Zeppelin only. It was expensive and inaccurate, though considerable damage was done and some casualties inflicted on the civilian population. An attempt was made by the Germans to pretend that they were bombing military targets, but in fact it was the civilian population's morale that was their primary objective. The Zeppelin was defeated by the end of 1916, and between May 1917 and May of the following year aeroplanes took over. There were many raids on the capital and other cities which caused quite heavy damage, and proportionately very heavy casualties; in all 1,414 persons were killed and 3,416 wounded. The effect on morale was also quite serious. Scenes approaching panic sometimes occurred. There were stampedes into London's underground railway tubes and other shelters and on one occasion an AA gun crew was almost lynched by an angry mob in Hyde Park because they refused to fire on a plane overhead that was, in fact, British: night raids held up the production of munitions: and over two hundred fighter planes, urgently needed on the Western Front in March of 1918, were kept in Britain to protect and encourage the civilian population. Very few German planes were shot down before the late spring of 1918.

When it is realised that all this was achieved by a numerically very insignificant German bomber force,

Early barrage balloon test over the Tower of London

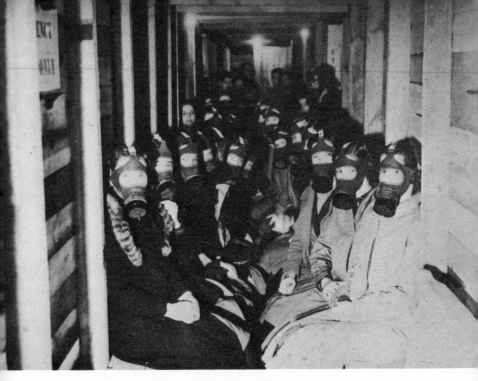

the 3rd Bombing Squadron, that in only one raid, the last, were more than thirty bombers sent over, and that these carried only a small load of light bombs, it is not surprising that both sides foresaw a tremendous, and perhaps an overwhelming, future for this type of warfare.

Had the war lasted into 1919 the RAF, which had already carried out a number of raids on German industrial towns, was planning to launch very heavy attacks of this sort on a very large scale. It seems probable, to judge by the effects of the comparatively light raids already made by the Independent Force, RAF, that the results would have been impressive both on German production and on morale.

Such, in very brief summary, was the story of bombing in 1914–18, and its effects were to be studied with great attention by the experts during the next two decades. Let us see what conclusions the policy-makers and the soldiers drew from the lessons of 1914–18.

Above: Office workers rehearse their air raid procedure. *Right:* Relaxed atmosphere at an Auxiliary Fire Service post

The more perspicacious airmen decided that the key to victory in the next war lay with the air fleets. An exponent of these views in their most extreme form was the Italian, General Douhet, who published his thesis, *The Command of the Air*, as early as 1921. His argument, briefly, was that a bomber force, if properly handled, could knock out an enemy power in a matter of weeks or even days. He did not believe that anti-aircraft guns or fighters could prevent the bombers from attacking and destroying the 'nerve centres' of the opponent's homeland – his railway junctions, ports, key factories and so on – and he stated that the only defence against bombing was counter-bombing.

'Air power is a weapon superlatively adapted to offensive operations, because it strikes suddenly and gives the enemy no time to parry the blow. . . . The aeroplane is not adaptable to defence, being pre-eminently an offensive weapon . . . There is no practical way to prevent the enemy from attacking us with his air force except to destroy his air power before he has a chance to strike at us. . . *We must . . . resign ourselves to the offensives the enemy inflicts upon us, while striving to put all our resources to work to inflict even heavier ones upon him. . .*' (General Douhet's italics.)

Such was one essential theory of the use of air power: a tremendous blow given at the earliest possible stage to destroy the enemy's air potential, followed by a succession of hammer blows, also of great violence, delivered against his cities, with objectives his industries, his communications and above all his civilian morale. It was calculated that ten planes, each carrying two tons of incendiaries, high-explosives and poison gas, could destroy everything within a circle of 500 metres diameter: to annihilate a city centre measuring three kilometres each way, or roughly the size of the City of London with the Whitehall district, only one attack by a force of 360 bombers would be needed. Thus the next war might be decided by tremendous aerial bombing during the first few days. This theory of the 'knock-out blow' remained, and still remains, an essential element of air force planning against future war.

In Britain the Air Staff, in the words of Mr Basil Collier, foresaw the coming war as 'a slogging match between rival bomber forces', and by the early thirties were fully converted to the view that only large-scale offensive bomber action from well-guarded bases could provide Great Britain with the necessary air

Right: A London family tries out the newly issued gas masks. *Far right:* Foretaste of the Blitz; damage from a Zeppelin raid on London in 1915

superiority that would bring victory. It was not, of course, possible for any British Government in the 'twenties or 'thirties to plan, or build, a bomber force capable of delivering a 'knock-out blow' to a potential enemy. The Air Staff therefore worked to build an air force which could parry the enemy's knock-out blow and could then be expanded to defeat that enemy by what came later to be called 'strategic' bombing. But the emphasis, at least until the autumn of 1938, was still very much upon bombers rather than fighters, and twice as much effort was put into the British bomber programme as went into the fighters.

Since no country could afford to keep 'standing patrols' of fighters in the air along its frontiers and coasts, the only hope of defeating bombers by fighters lay in identifying the enemy's course and probable objective at a considerable distance from his target and then converging the airborne defence against the attacking force. This would vastly multiply the efficacy of the individual fighter. But in 1932 no such identification appeared possible. It was obvious, as Mr Baldwin then stated in the House of Commons, that 'the bomber would always get through'.

The picture began to change in the mid-1930s, with the introduction of the radar chain. By 1938 it was becoming plain that the early information supplied by the radar stations on the coast did offer a chance of parrying the enemy's bomber attack by fighter intervention. It was therefore once again considered worthwhile to re-orientate British defensive strategy about the radar chain and the new eight-gun fighter, which combination, indeed, won the Battle of Britain. But that, of course, still lay hidden in the future. Furthermore, though it was no longer believed that

the bomber would always get through, it was taken for granted that quite a number of bombers would, particularly by night, and that London would be bombed. So the various British governments still had to plan against this contingency. If there were to be a second world war, and their military advisers were to have judged correctly – as they must assume they had – what then would be the effects of the 'knock-out blow' on London and other primary targets? The answer, also supplied by experts, was an excessively depressing one.

The total weight of bombs dropped by the Germans on Britain during the war of 1914–18 had amounted to some 300 tons, which had caused almost 5,000 casualties, of which one third were fatal, giving a figure of sixteen per ton of bombs. But the two big daylight raids on London had caused 832 casualties, or 121 per ton, while the sixteen night raids of 1917–18 had caused fifty-two per ton dropped. As early as 1924, therefore, the Air

Staff reckoned that casualties in a future war would be in the nature of fifty per ton of bombs, one third of which would be fatal. In 1934 the Air Staff, using the still illegal German Air Force as their basis of calculation, reckoned that in the foreseeable future the Luftwaffe, were it to operate from bases in the Low Countries, could drop 150 tons of bombs on Britain daily for an unspecified period. In 1938 the Committee of Imperial Defence anticipated 3,500 tons of bombs on London, delivered by 'planes based on Germany, within the first twenty-four hours of attack, followed by 600 tons per day. The figure of fifty casualties per ton was still accepted and, indeed, seemed to be confirmed by reports received from Spain. In April, 1939, the Air Staff, while adhering to the figure of 3,500 tons for the 'knock-out blow', now believed that the Germans could increase their daily bombing to 700 tons and that by April 1940 the figure would be 950 tons per day dropped by

some 800 aircraft based in Germany. The Ministry of Health, using these figures which forecast 600,000 killed and 1,200,000 wounded in the first six months, estimated that between 1,000,000 and 2,800,000 hospital beds would be needed for the injured, depending on the length of their stay in hospital. And there it may be of interest, for purposes of comparison, to point out that during the entire blitz of September 1940 – May 1941, London had some 90,000 casualties, of whom just under 20,000 were killed and 25,000 seriously injured; during this period 18,000 tons of bombs were dropped, which, by the 1937 estimate, should have killed over 280,000 civilians. But gas, of course, was not used. The estimate was thus an over-estimate by fourteen-fold.

And the expectation of horror did not end with casualties, though these are perhaps the easiest yard-stick. In late 1938 it was estimated that 500,000 houses would be totally destroyed or rendered uninhabitable by bombing, and that between one and two millions would be seriously damaged. It was believed that the public services would almost certainly break down. Panic on a nation-wide scale was feared. In London, conditions would be horrible beyond belief. During the winter of 1917–18 more than 10,000 people used to crowd into a single tube station for shelter, and on one occasion in February of 1918 almost a third of a million Londoners sought refuge in the tubes. In the incomparably worse bombings now expected, these figures would be much greater. It was feared that the populace would crowd into the tubes, where there were no provisions for food or sanitation, and would refuse to come out. The medical authorities had no doubt that severe epidemics would break out as a result. Apart from disease, madness on a huge

scale was expected. In 1939 the Mental Health Emergency Committee reported that psychiatric casualties might exceed the physical by three to one: that is to say, between three and four millions of people would suffer from hysteria or other acute neurotic conditions. It would not even be possible to bury the dead properly, since it would be beyond the resources of the country to provide the necessary timber for coffins. Mass burial in lime pits was envisaged, or even the dumping of bodies from hoppers into the Channel. However, with the city on fire above-ground, the few roads still open crowded with hysterical refugees, and the tubes crammed with starving, panic-stricken masses prey to virulent epidemics, it is hard to see how the corpses could even have been conveyed to the pits.

Such then, at its blackest, was the picture that confronted the Government when it considered the next war, and when it set out to lessen the degree of catastrophe it anticipated,

A Zeppelin is brought down in 1916, and sentries place the wreckage under heavy guard

it found itself dealing with a nation which contemplated a future war with emotions ranging from terror to apathy. The working class, massacred in 1914–18, cheated, as it thought, out of the promised fruits of victory, lied to by its popular press, and later plunged into the hopeless quagmire of mass unemployment, not unnaturally regarded the governing class with deep suspicion and dislike. Why should *we* fight for *them?* was the simple basis of working-class pacifism, which was given an idealistic *raison d'être* by such popular figures as Lansbury and Dr Salter. The Labour Party was not solidly pacifist by any means, and after Hitler had come to power in Germany several of its leaders, some of whom had even gone to prison as conscientious objectors during the First World War, realised that it might be necessary to defend Britain's political liberties by force of arms. But it had a very strong pacifist wing, and most Socialists were, in general, far less interested in international affairs than in the class struggle at home.

The middle classes were as usual curiously silent and it is hard to generalise about their attitude, since for the last two generations fatalism seems to have been a major ingredient of their point of view, save during brief periods of national or social crisis. They were prepared to follow the Government, even into war, but the fact that some two million members of this class evacuated themselves, at their own expense, from their homes in the cities when war was imminent shows that they shared the general terrified foreboding of what that war would bring. A proportion, probably small, of the middle and upper-middle classes believed that in view of Germany's military preponderance – which in practice meant Germany's ability to bomb Britain – we should accept her political preponderance as well, but the dislike of 'the Hun' instilled during the First World War was still very strong, and the out-

and-out appeasers-at-any-price were few, as were the Fascists who admired Hitler on so-called ideological grounds.

The two halves of the nation, divergent in their attitudes to war, also tended to distrust and fear one another. And the genesis of the ARP (Air Raid Precaution) services was, by a curious coincidence, closely connected with that distrust and fear.

When the first, very tentative, plans for Civil Defence were being discussed in the autumn of 1926, the organisational structure taken as a rough model was that which had been called into existence when the General Strike had threatened the country with chaos. That is to say, it was to be largely a voluntary organisation, whose members would therefore be men, and women, willing to accept responsibility, as had the Special Constables of 1926. Just as the 80,000 specials enrolled before the strike had increased to 200,000 in ten days, so it was hoped that a nucleus of ARP personnel would be able to draw on a similar type of volunteer, and expand rapidly should a crisis develop. This gave its whole tone to the British ARP services, and particularly to the Wardens' Service, in the years to come. Unlike the equivalent German service, it was never a para-military force: its discipline, as will be seen, was primarily that of moral pressure, and its members came largely from the middle classes. In Germany, where for example every concierge had certain duties and thus considerable authority within his building, the ARP service cut across all social distinctions. In England, relying as it did on volunteers, it remained, like all other voluntary work, primarily a middle-class activity, for most workers seldom volunteer and only reluctantly accept even the limited authority of an armband and a whistle. This, in months to come, was to have curious – and at times unfortunate – results in some purely working-class boroughs where there were few

Left: Rooftop fire-watch. *Above:*
Shopkeepers taped their windows to
reduce the effects of blast

volunteers and where the people
therefore sometimes felt pathetically
neglected and forgotten.

When it became plain from develop-
ments in strategic affairs that during
a future war London would be heavily,
and probably accurately, bombed at
least by night, the Government had to
make two plans. What could be done,
apart from strengthening the active
defences, before the bombing began:
and what must be done during and
after the raids?

An individual target could be hidden
from the enemy bombers by smoke and
camouflage during the day, and by a
total blackout after dark. So far as
London went, no daytime device could
hide the great city, though a lot of
time, and paint, was spent in colouring
factory chimneys and large buildings
a mottled green and buff. This did no

harm, paint was plentiful and the
broken outlines probably even gave
the workers a certain feeling of
confidence. Smoke-screens could be,
and later were, used to conceal certain
small vital targets, and the factories
were to be encouraged to burn fuel
which produced more smoke than was
permitted in peacetime. It was, of
course, not possible to blanket London
in a permanent fog: even had it been,
this would scarcely have been desir-
able, and in any case the enemy could
simply have dropped his bombs into it.
The blackout was another matter.
This was a legacy of the First World
War, when lights had been dimmed to
prevent the enemy from pinpointing
his targets. It was decided at an early
stage that in the coming war the blackout would be total, all over Britain and
Northern Ireland. This again was no
direct defence of London, but the
blackout, together with the guns and
balloons, did provide a certain protection in that it made it very difficult

17

Families were dispersed with brutal efficiency as the danger to London came closer. Thousands of children, ticketed for identification, were taken out to strange new homes in country areas

for night bombers to bomb accurately. Had they been able to do so, had the entire weight of each raid been concentrated against one or two boroughs, the casualties would undoubtedly have been heavier – comparable perhaps to the Coventry casualties, but repeated night after night – and above all the effect on civilian morale would have been far graver. More protection than this the blackout could not provide. But nevertheless, as will be seen, Londoners were to attach an almost mystical significance to its strict observation. Finally, the Government could and did ensure that the broadcasting and other wireless stations did not act as beacons to guide the enemy bombers to their targets. Still, London could not be hidden.

If it could not be hidden, and was hardly defensible, would it not be wiser to evacuate the entire population? This problem was first considered in 1933, but as late as September 1938 the plan was still a very rudimentary one. After the Munich crisis the question was examined seriously, and the plan was applied during the following year was agreed.

Government-sponsored evacuation should be limited, broadly speaking, to children, infants with their mothers, expectant mothers, and certain classes of invalids such as the blind: workers and others needed for the war effort were to be encouraged to stay at their places of work: the remainder of the population, many of whom were unflatteringly described as *bouches inutiles*, could go or stay as they pleased, at their own expense. Plans were made to evacuate the Government from London, if the need should arise, but millions of Londoners would still have to face the bombs. The first provision that the Government made for their safety, and one

Primitive early-war communications system. A policeman on bicycle patrol indicates the 'all-clear'. Later a system of sirens was used

which corresponded to the degree of fear this menace inspired, was to give the population the maximum protection against gas. In 1934 defence against gas, namely the production of respirators and anti-gas clothing and the purchase of bleach powder and medical supplies, was financially the largest single item of civil defence. In 1936 plans for the distribution of respirators to all civilians were accepted, and during the Munich crisis, gas-masks were issued to almost the entire population. Apart from the digging of trenches, this was almost all that the Government could do for the people during that autumn. It was psychologically a very wise move. To possess at least something, some object, for their own protection even if it were only a respirator, made a great difference, as was shown by the outcry when it was discovered that there were not enough anti-gas helmets for all the babies.

One aspect, then, of the ARP services was tackled, and at great expense dealt with, once and for all as it turned out, before ever the war began.

In popular estimation the next greatest menace after gas was high-explosive. Fire, which in fact did far more damage than high-explosive, came a poor third. In providing shelter from high-explosive bombs the Government's policy, though it was to prove in general wise, did not, as with the anti-gas precautions, quite correspond with what the people demanded.

As already stated, raids were expected to take the form of short, violent onslaughts, the most violent being the first, delivered at the rate of one or more a day, either by day or by night. It was considered for planning purposes that the average warning period, between the bombers crossing the coast and the bombs actually dropping, would be some seven minutes. It was feared, indeed expected, that the people would panic. The Government's policy was, there- fore, to disperse the shelters. There were two principal reasons for this. If huge communal shelters were built, the so-called 'deep shelters' which were the only ones giving full protection even against direct hits, they would have to be fairly widely spaced. It would then take most of the shelterers more than seven minutes to reach them; they would be caught in the street, and the casualties would be heavy. Also after one or two experiences of this sort, it was feared that a 'deep-shelter mentality' would develop, that is, that many people would go down into the shelters and refuse to come out. This would not only produce feeding, medical, and sanitary problems that were almost insoluble, but would also paralyse the industrial life of London. Crowded shelters, besides being a perfect breeding place for various physical infections, would encourage every form of mass hysteria from defeatism to panic. A subsidiary consideration which influenced the Government against the building of deep shelters was the vast expense. For the purpose of dispersal, therefore, Anderson shelters – those curved-roof, kennel-like constructions of corrugated steel which could protect four or six people from the effects of a near miss – were issued free on a very large scale to the poor, and at a nominal charge of £7 to those who could afford to pay. These were to be half-sunk into backyards, and, as it turned out, provided adequate protection against almost anything save a direct hit. But in the East End many streets consisted of back-to-back cottages and there was thus nowhere to put the Anderson. In those old and often rickety houses attempts to reinforce a ground-floor room with steel supports were not likely to provide much protection. Brick street shelters, originally intended for passers-by caught in a sudden raid, were built in such streets, but these did not look, and indeed, as will be seen, were not always very safe. Besides, many people wanted to go under-

22 T	17 T	17 T	INCLUDING LARD AND DRIPPING 12	INCLUDING LARD AND DRIPPING 7 T	INCLUDING LARD DRIP
MEAT 23 T	T 18	MEAT 18 T	MEAT 13	MEAT 13	OKING FATS INCLUDING LARD AND DRIPPING 8	COOKIN INCLU LARD DRIP T
MEAT 24 T	T 19	MEAT 19 T	T 14	MEAT 14 T	OKING FATS INCLUDING LARD AND DRIPPING 9	COOKIN INCL LARD DRI T
MEAT 25 T	T 20	MEAT 20 T	T 15	MEAT 15 T	OKING FATS INCLUDING LARD AND DRIPPING 10	COOKIN INCL LARD DRI T
MEAT 26 T	T 21	MEAT 21 T	T 16	MEAT 16 T	OKING FATS INCLUDING LARD AND DRIPPING 11	COOKIN INCL LARD DRI

AGE 1.—MEAT.   TRAVELLER R.B. 3.

OKI
INCL
LAR
DRI

nsumer's Name (BLOCK LETTERS)

HIS MAJESTY THE KING

ddress BUCKINGHAM PALACE
(BLOCK LETTERS)

LONDON, S.W.1   CA   57001

16 January 1940

ground. That is what they had done in 1918, and that is what they were determined to do again. They felt happier, and therefore safer, in crowded cellars or tubes. And even when the bombing began, and it was proved over and over again that many of the tubes were not safe and that shelters beneath the railway arches were often death-traps, a fairly large proportion of East Enders still preferred the quite illusory sense of security engendered by being in a crowded place.

The Government was determined that this time the tubes would not be used for shelter. Not only were many of them very unsafe against the new and powerful bombs, but there was also the danger of flooding. And, finally, if the city above ground were a holocaust, the tubes would provide the quickest and easiest means of transportation and communication. As will be shown, public pressure proved too great and the authorities had to give way on this point when the time came.

The organisation of the ARP services in London remained more or less unaltered throughout the Blitz of the following year. England was divided into Regions, of which there were nine, and of those the London Region was geographically the smallest. It contained a pre-war population of almost nine millions and stretched from Tilbury in the east to Windsor in the west, from Biggin Hill in the south to a point near St Albans in the north. The Regional Headquarters were in the Geological Museum, Exhibition Road, South Kensington.

Beneath the Region was the Group Headquarters. Each Group contained a number of boroughs, and its primary task was to move needed reinforcements when a borough was unable to deal with air attack from its own resources. The borough was the tactical unit of Civil Defence, and each had its own Report and Control Centre, usually in the Town Hall. The borough was divided into districts, which might contain as many as 10,000 persons each.

The basic unit was the Wardens' Post. Each Post was manned by from three to six wardens. In theory there were to be approximately ten Posts to the square mile, and each Post looked after an area containing some 500 persons: in practice some Posts were much larger, some smaller. The Wardens were the backbone of the ARP services. Before the raids began it was their task to issue gas-masks, see that the blackout was enforced, and generally instruct the public. When the raids began, their duty, in theory at least, was principally to pass on information. Each Post was equipped with a telephone, supplemented by runners. The Warden patrolling the two or three blocks of his 'sector' would see a bomb drop, and would assess the nature of the damage and the assistance needed from the specialised services. He would then make his report to the Control Centre, who would send out the specialised services at their disposal – a Stretcher Party, or a Decontamination Squad in the event of gas, or a Rescue Unit to dig out men or women trapped in the rubble. If there was fire they would pass the information to the Fire Service, which had its own hierarchy under the London County Council. If ambulances were needed – they were also administered by the LCC – these would be sent. Finally there were the Heavy Rescue, or Demolition Squads, another LCC organisation consisting mostly of men drawn from the building trade and equipped with the necessary gear for dealing with major demolitions. In practice, of course, the Wardens often had to act as firemen, rescue men and male nurses. And after the raid was over it was they who guided the homeless to the Rest Centres, who helped people find their property among the

In democratic wartime Britain, even royalty shared the rigours of rationing

ruins, who arranged the evacuation of buildings threatened by unexploded bombs, and who performed a thousand other tasks of every variety. A Government publication of 1938, *The Duties of Air Raid Wardens*, had said: 'In time of war, an air raid warden should regard himself, first and foremost, as a member of the public chosen and trained to be a leader of his fellow-citizens and, with them and for them, to do the right thing in an emergency.' The great majority of Wardens were unpaid volunteers, who did a full day's work before reporting at the Posts. Only some 16,000 London Wardens – out of some 200,000 – were full-time and paid, at the not very handsome rate of £3 per week. A number were women. The Wardens, and the firemen, were to be the true heroes of the Blitz.

Such were the preparations made to meet the bomb attack which it was anticipated would immediately follow the outbreak of war. In fact the Germans not only did not launch the massive air attack on London on 3rd September 1939, but do not even seem to have made any plans for such an attack at this time. In his General Directive No. 1 for the prosecution of the war, dated 31st August 1939, Hitler laid down: 'The decision regarding attack on London rests with me', and more than a year was to pass before the decision was taken. True, the air raid warning went at once that morning, but the invader was no more than a single French civilian plane which arrived, unheralded, from France, and the warnings had been sounded as a result. This was not, however, immediately realised even by Londoners, who had been taught to believe that the moment war broke out the Luftwaffe would 'raze' London to the ground. They could hardly be expected to know that the Luftwaffe staff had never intended to do any such thing.

During the first ten months of the

Field-Marshal Kesselring

war, then, there was no German plan for the bombing of London. Such an operation was, of course, discussed, but dismissed, and Hitler hoped that the fear of bombing alone would cause the British to surrender. Should they eventually fail to do so, terror would then bring them to their knees. But this was the final trump, which must not be played prematurely.

That the fear was very great, in September of 1939, cannot be denied. Lord Baldwin, speaking in Parliament in October 1938, had stated that had war come at the time of the Munich crisis, 'there would have been tens of thousands of mangled people – citizens, women and children – before a single soldier or sailor gave his life for his country. That is an awful thought.' It is indeed, despite its phrasing. A woman, questioned by Mass Observation on 2nd September 1939, that is to say the day before war broke out, said: 'Felt sick at news. Feeling that we'd be for it at once. Woke at three and lay waiting for bombs till time to get up.' Yet on 4th and 5th September, though the citizens of London might still glance apprehensively at the skies, they were, apart from the large number run over in the blackout, quite unmangled. For almost half the Luftwaffe was busy at the other end of Europe, and London was preparing for the attack that did not yet come. Because the mass bombing had failed to materialise, their preparations enjoyed only a modest success. A million and a half mothers and children were evacuated from the cities with, in general, remarkable smoothness but by the end of the year, of the million and a half who had left the cities, one million – including almost all the mothers – had returned. By May of 1940 only an estimated quarter of a million children were still living in their wartime foster homes. The long-planned evacuation, on which the Government had set so much store, had been a failure.

Another sort of evacuation was more successful. Something over two million people hurried out of London, under their own steam or in their own motor-cars, as soon as war broke out. Many of them stayed away, and *The Times* was to write, in early 1941, of country hotels 'filled with well-to-do refugees, who too often have fled from nothing. They sit and read and knit and eat and drink . . .' It was undoubtedly an excellent thing that London was rid of these people when it faced the bombs. They would only have been in the way, and they presumably spent a pleasant, if boring, war in their country hotels.

In London, during these months of phoney war, the chief discomfort was undoubtedly the blackout, which to begin with was total, not even torches being allowed in the streets. As the days grew shorter, travelling to and from work in the dark became a protracted and exhausting nightmare. It was dangerous too, and the number of road casualties rose sharply, until in December these amounted to no less than forty casualties to pedestrians per day. In January the Government was compelled slightly to relax their more stringent rules, which had been frequently enforced with an absurd rigidity. Throughout the country one and a half million Anderson shelters had been distributed free, more were on the way, and if in early 1940 there was any London household which did not possess such a shelter, that was not the fault of the Government. The trenches that had been dug in the parks a year before were roofed, revetted and enlarged. The borough councils declared a number of basements and other apparently sturdy edifices public shelters, and proceeded to reinforce those that had need of such support. The public had not been informed that they were not to be be prevented from using the tubes as shelters, but a number of tube stations in central London were closed so that bulkheads could be installed which, when shut, would prevent flooding. Brick and concrete surface shelters, each to hold fifty people, were rapidly

constructed. In fact by the end of the year the Government's arrangements for shelter on the dispersal system were largely completed in the London Region. Apart from the Andersons, public shelters of one sort or another to hold over 800,000 people were ready or nearing completion.

A great many men and women volunteered for the ARP services, over one and a half million throughout Britain, and the London services were up to strength. The boroughs had over 9,000 paid Wardens and over 10,000 whole-time members of Stretcher Parties. The Rescue Services were well organised and contained 12,000 paid members. Recruiting for the Auxiliary Fire Service was going on satisfactorily, and sixty per cent of the war establishment of pumps and other equipment had been issued. The rest was produced by the summer. Report and control centres had been set up in schools and other commandeered buildings. It all went remarkably smoothly, and in view of the enormity of the task the authorities were remarkably efficient.

The main task now was to instruct the public as to what they should do in the event of raids, and this proved difficult for two reasons: the invincible stupidity and frivolity of a large portion of the public, and the growing unpopularity of the ARP services, and particularly of the Wardens, whose jobs it was to give the public that instruction.

Not that the lessons the public had to learn were in any way difficult or complicated. A Public Information Leaflet, issued to every household at the beginning of the war, stated in heavy type: IF YOU THROW A BUCKET OF WATER ON A BURNING INCENDIARY BOMB, IT WILL EXPLODE AND THROW BURNING FRAGMENTS IN ALL DIRECTIONS. The leaflet went on to say how these bombs should be smothered in sand or with a sandbag. It all seems simple enough. Yet in late 1939 Mass Observation reported that only one-third of the persons interviewed in London could give a correct answer when asked how incendiaries should be dealt with. The commonest incorrect answer was, 'to throw the bomb into water', or 'to throw water over the bomb'. Other recorded answers included:

'Stand up by a brick wall.'
'Lay on it.'
'Leave it to a Warden.'
'Flop a coat over it, or throw it into a sewer, or anywhere there is water.'
'Pick it up and run it in water.'
'Sit back and hold tight.'
'Leave it where it is and run.'
'Keep the thin places of your house patched up.'
'Put on your gas-mask.'

Most people did not bother to read this or any other of the Public Information Leaflets. Some even regarded them as an obscure insult. One person described his reaction to them as one of 'contemptuous and cynical amusement'.

The most obvious target for this developing cynicism was the Wardens. There they were, sitting about all day, being apparently paid for doing nothing, and, what is more, trying to tell *us* what to do in the event of raids that will never happen.

They were even attacked, as early as October, as 'slackers and parasites' in the House of Commons, and in January the establishment was cut down, and a number of the paid Wardens dismissed as a result. What is surprising is that so very high a proportion should have remained at their posts, continued their remarkably uninspiring training, and thus have been able to carry out their function so efficiently and bravely when the time came.

There was, in fact a dull resentment against the war as a whole that steadily increased throughout that boring and mildly uncomfortable winter.

And so the phoney war went on. The theatres and cinemas, that had all been closed by order, gradually reopened. Rationing, always a thoroughly popular measure with the British since it appeals to the egalitarianism of some and the notorious 'sense of fair play' of others, was introduced and adjudged an immediate success. The popularity of the Minister for Food, Lord Woolton, reached heights only equalled by the unpopularity of his equally hardworked colleague, the Home Secretary and Minister for Home Security, Sir John Anderson. The men and women of the Civil Defence services continued to train for an eventuality which the majority now believed would never come. The war became known as the Bore War. And the Air Ministry staff increased their estimate of the danger hanging over London's head. The Germans, they now calculated, could drop 2,000 tons of bombs per day for several days, and 700 tons for an unlimited period. They still estimated the probable casualty rate at fifty per ton dropped.

The bombing of Rotterdam was the awakening. When the Germans invaded the Low Countries, on 10th May they again employed the blitzkrieg tactics which had served them so well in Poland. This operation, unlike the others, was not immediately and entirely successful. General Student, commanding the airborne troops, was held up in Rotterdam. He asked for air support on a large scale. This was given him on 13th May, large areas of Rotterdam were flattened, and many civilians killed. Churchill was to refer to this operation as 'a massacre', and to the Western World as a whole it seemed at that time, and later, a terror attack of the sort that had long been awaited. It also appeared to have achieved the purpose of such attacks, for on the next day the Dutch army laid down its arms.

There was no other example of the massive bombing of a civilian target during the Western Campaign, though small forces of German bombers did raid towns in central and southern France with the obvious purpose of inspiring terror in their inhabitants. In this objective they were to a large degree successful. Dread of what the Luftwaffe might do contributed power fully to the demoralisation of the French. This dread was at least partially responsible for the speed with which the French Government surrendered as soon as the French armies were defeated.

Britain was clearly the next on the list, and in June of 1940 the Luftwaffe, now busy installing itself on a great semi-circle of airfields all within easy striking distance of Britain, looked a truly formidable force. It was.

And yet somehow the almost panic terror of 1938 and the less hysterical but perhaps more deep-rooted fears of 1939 hardly re-appeared. The reason for this was twofold. Most important was the new mood of the country, a mood most skilfully tempered and

He-111s in formation over England

welded by the new Prime Minister Winston Churchill. knew too much about war to confuse forecast with fact. He made no bones about the grimness of the immediate future, but he did not believe that Britain would be conquered. Nor did the British people. They had no first-hand knowledge of defeat and, being a remarkably unimaginative people, have never been able to conceive of it as more than a theoretical possibility. His determination and their stubbornness during that summer were admirably suited. Sir Winston Churchill has drawn a very clear picture of his own attitude in his *History of the Second World War*. That of the people whom he led. is depicted in Peter Fleming's *Invasion 1940*.

And the word 'invasion' is the key to the second reason for the change of attitude of the country. Hitherto massive bombing had had, as it were, all the publicity. That was the threat,

that was the danger. But now it was equalled if not surpassed in the popular mind by the menace of invasion. And against this there was something that every man and woman could do. In October of 1938 and September of 1939 the British, and particularly the Londoners, had envisaged their role in the expected catastrophe as almost entirely a passive one. Huddling in shelters, groping their way through clouds of poisonous gases, dying in the streets, victims. Now, in July of 1940, though they once again expected heavy raids, they saw themselves in another role as well: hurling home-made grenades at German tanks, garrotting Nazi paratroopers in the night; in a word, fighting. Churchill's blood-curdling phrase, 'You can always take one with you', struck a responsive chord. And so the bombing was seen only as a part of the forthcoming battle, not as the final cataclysm.

The grumbling and the whining stopped, almost overnight, and few people paid much attention to those voices which, like gramophone records stuck in one groove, were unable to stop uttering words no longer suited to the country's mood. The Socialists had entered the Churchill Government: the country was united as it has seldom been: this was the period of the 'Dunkirk spirit'. People ceased throwing boots at Wardens, and were now only too anxious to see that their neighbours, and they themselves, blacked out their houses. Many of those who had withdrawn from the Civil Defence Services volunteered again. Millions joined the Home Guard. And the country's eyes were fixed on the air battle which began in August, and which has gone down to history as the Battle of Britain.

As is known, the German objective during the Battle of Britain was the destruction of the Royal Air Force as a preliminary to the invasion, and for the time being Hitler had decreed that London was not to be bombed. But on 24th August a chain of events began which gave Hitler justification for rescinding that decree. On that day a few German planes accidentally, and against Hitler's orders, dropped bombs on London. Churchill was quick to order reprisals. On the very next night eighty-one aircraft of Bomber Command were sent to bomb Berlin. They did little damage. But for the next week the British bombers were over Berlin whenever the weather permitted. This is turn gave Hitler the perfect excuse for reprisals. On 4th September he announced that he intended to wipe out the British cities. On 5th September the appropriate orders were issued for the attack on London. This time the bait, if it was still bait, had been taken. And on 6th September Göring arrived on the Channel Coast to take direct command of the battle of London, a battle in which that inflated personage hoped to win everlasting glory in Valhalla and, incidentally, to end the war.

The Blitz begins

On that Saturday afternoon Göring and Kesselring are said to have stood on the cliffs of Cap Gris Nez and watched the bombers of 2nd Air Fleet form up and set off for London, while the escorting fighters took up their positions above and below the Heinkels and Dorniers. That was at approximately four o'clock. Further to the south bomber after bomber of Sperrle's 3rd Air Fleet, forming the second wave of the attack, roared along the runways of Normandy and Brittany and was airborne. That afternoon well over 300 bombers, escorted by about 600 fighters, flew against London. The attack achieved surprise. Fighter Command Headquarters at Stanmore and Air-Marshal Park's No. 11 Group at Uxbridge covering the approaches to the metropolis did not expect a concentrated attack on London yet. They had every reason to assume that the Luftwaffe would continue its successful raids on the sector-stations, and the fighter squadrons were therefore sent up to intercept such attacks.

Indeed, had the Luftwaffe been assigned its targets by the German air-marshal, that is almost certainly what the Luftwaffe would have done. But this operation had been ordered by Hitler and was under Göring's control. Military logic was thus at a discount and surprise was achieved. If it was a strategic blunder – and it is just conceivable that this switching of the bomber fleets to London lost Germany the war – it was a tactical triumph.

The illogicality confused and misled the British Chiefs of Staff. They had assumed, quite correctly as we know, that the German plan for invasion would involve a heavy attack on London immediately before the troop-carrying barges put to sea. Air reconnaissance had revealed that the German preparations in the Channel ports were nearly completed. When, therefore, the Chiefs of Staff, who were actually meeting that afternoon, heard the crashing of the bombs on London and learned that the great attack so long awaited was in fact

Germany's air attack on Britain begins, and Göring and his staff watch across the Dover Straits

being delivered on the capital, they reckoned that the invasion was likely to take place within a matter of hours. They therefore issued the code word 'Cromwell' to commands on that same evening. 'Cromwell' meant 'invasion imminent'. They could not be expected to guess at this early hour that the real meaning of the attack was to be exactly the reverse. Hitler, dissatisfied with the results achieved by his airmen and increasingly irritated by the technical advice he was receiving from his sailors and soldiers, was switching to those methods of terror and brutality which had hitherto won him such spectacular victories both in his own country and abroad. The London docks were, of course, a first-class military target, and in this respect the attack on them was fully justified from a military point of view, at least on a long-term basis; for had they been put out of operation, together with Southampton, Bristol and Liverpool, it would certainly have been very difficult, and might have

proved impossible, for Britain to continue the war. But all this was far removed from the tactical requirements of the German sailors and soldiers waiting to carry out Operation 'Sealion'. Furthermore, it is hard not to believe that Hitler, in making the long-delayed decision to bomb a target in the middle of London, was not also indulging in that taste for sadism and destruction which was such a marked aspect of his character. But that is speculative and not of great importance. What is important is that the attack on the docks meant a basic switch of German strategy, away from 'Sealion' which then seemed imminent, to a long-range attack on Britain's communications as a whole and on the morale of the civilian inhabitants of Britain's capital city. Strategically it was a political act of violence. That is why it took the British soldiers and airmen by surprise for half an hour or so.

The first wave came in from the east, with targets the docks below Tower Bridge, Woolwich Arsenal and again the oil installations farther down river. The Thames and Medway guns opened up on the leading formations, flying westwards, at about five o'clock. A quarter of an hour later the first bombs fell on Woolwich Arsenal – a prime military target – and damaged two important factories as well. Other squadrons went on to bomb West Ham, Poplar, Stepney and Bermondsey, the riverside boroughs on either side of the Thames' great double meander where are concentrated the Victoria and Albert Docks, the West India Docks and the vast Surrey Commercial Docks. Having reached their objectives, they turned away to the north, and now they were in their turn attacked by some seven fighter squadrons of Nos 11 and 12 Groups. They were roughly handled, but their bombs had exploded where they meant them to, and already fires were starting. Meanwhile the second wave was driving for the capital from the south and southeast. Some of these were intercepted by the RAF fighters before reaching the capital, and one squadron fought a running fight over London. In general, however, the Messerschmitts managed to blast a way through for their bombers and the target area was again heavily hit. The bombs, over 300 tons of high explosive and many thousands of incendiaries, rained down not only on the docks, but also on the mean, closely packed and highly inflammable rows of little streets that housed the workers and their families. In an hour and a half London received its heaviest daylight raid of the war, and its most concentrated. Though bombs were dropped as far away as Tottenham and Croydon, it was the East End that bore the brunt of it. By half past six that evening whole streets of little two-storey cottages, built as cheaply and

quickly as the speculative builders of the 19th century could put them up, had collapsed in dust and rubble. To the countryman or the town planner, those grimy, aged, jerry-built dwellings might be nothing but slums, and in retrospect it is often said that the action of the Luftwaffe was comparable to that of the surgeon's knife, removing once and for all a cancerous growth. But for those who lived in those dreary, dirty streets, these cottages and shops and pubs were home. At half past six many of those homes no longer existed. And the fires were only just beginning to catch hold.

Nor was there any chance of extinguishing them before darkness fell, when they would provide a tremendous beacon to draw new bomber formations, with fresh loads of high explosives and incendiaries. During this biggest daylight raid the Germans lost over forty aircraft, but the RAF, already stretched almost to snapping point, had lost twenty-eight fighters and seventeen pilots it could ill afford. And the East End was ablaze. Göring might well congratulate himself on a victory. He did so, with his customary ostentation, that same evening, over the German wireless.

The blaze, as the sun sank towards the west, was enormous and visible for miles. From every part of London eyes were turned towards the Isle of Dogs. Mr Maxwell-Hyslop, who worked at what was then the Board of Education, has said:

'We'd been down to Richmond to tea with some friends. We came back on bicycles at about five o'clock and we saw this enormous great mushroom of smoke. It was so big, and towered up in the sky so high, that one couldn't believe it was smoke at all, and for a long time we didn't know what it could be. We'd heard the guns going and we'd heard the sirens going but we never dreamt of anything like this. And then we got up to the top of this rise in Richmond Park and we could see this smoke, this column of smoke,

and we said – My goodness, that must be somewhere near Hammersmith. And then we bicycled on, and we said – Well, it must be Chelsea. And finally when we got home, it was only then that we realised it was ten or twelve miles away from us still. And then we went up on the roof of our flat and saw this great horizon plainly, this red column of smoke towering up into the sky, a terrifying sight.'

Nearer to the fires, the Dean of St Paul's, Dr Matthews, was on duty that evening. 'Inside the Cathedral', he has written, 'the light was such that I have never seen the stained-glass windows glow as they did then.'

At about eight o'clock that evening the German night bombers took off from their bases again, and a little less than an hour later, as darkness fell and the fires blazed more fiercely, the first bombs were dropped into the holocaust. All London wondered what was happening beneath that pall of twisting, crimson, oily smoke.

The historian of the London Fire

Bomber crews are briefed for an operation

Brigade has written, in *Front Line*:

'Four-fifths of the firemen involved had had no prior experience of actual fire-fighting. In normal times a 30-pump fire is a very big fire. Shortly after midnight there were nine fires in London rating over 100 pumps. In the Surrey docks there were two, of 300 and 130 pumps; at Woolwich Arsenal, 200 pumps; at Bishopsgate Goods Yard and at five points on the docks, 100-pump fires. All these were technically "out of hand", that is to say unsurrounded, uncontrolled and spreading. In Quebec Yard, Surrey Docks, was the night's biggest fire – immense in its area, moving with disconcerting speed, generating terrific heat. It was thirty or forty times bigger than the great Barbican fire of 1938, the biggest in London's recent history. It set alight the wooden blocks in the roadways, a thing without precedent. A blaze covering

33

such an area is not only worse than a smaller one in direct proportion to its area, but is far harder to fight than its mere extent would suggest. The greater the cumulative heat, the fiercer the draught of cold air dragged in to feed it, and thus the quicker the movement of the fire and the greater the length of its flames. They were so long and their heat so great as to blister the paint on fireboats that tried to slip past under the lee of the opposite river bank 300 yards away. Solid embers a foot long were tossed into streets afar off to start fresh fires. Stocks of timber which the firemen had drenched began at once to steam, then to dry, then themselves to burst into flame in the intense heat radiated from nearby blazes.

'While the men fought this monstrous fire, the enemy continued to drop bombs into it, throughout the night. Time and again these would re-kindle an area that had just been laboriously conquered. Only with daybreak could real progress begin. The exhausted men could not be relieved after a normal interval because the brigades were fully extended. Many fireman were at work here for forty hours, some officers for longer. Such was the baptism of fire of most of London's wartime firemen.

'At Woolwich Arsenal men fought the flames among boxes of live ammunition and crates of nitro-glycerine, under a hail of bombs directed at London's number one military target. But in the docks themselves strange things were going on. There were pepper fires, loading the surrounding air heavily with stinging particles, so that when the firemen took a deep breath it felt like burning fire itself. There were rum fires, with torrents of blazing liquid pouring from the warehouse doors and barrels exploding like bombs themselves. There was a paint fire, another cascade of white-hot flame, coating the pumps with varnish that could be not cleaned for weeks. A rubber fire gave forth black clouds of smoke so asphyxiating that it could only be fought from a distance, and was always threatening to choke the attackers. Sugar, it seems, burns well in liquid form as it floats on the water in dockland basins. Tea makes a blaze that is "sweet, sickly and very intense". One man found it odd to be pouring cold water on hot tea leaves. A grain warehouse when burning produced great clouds of black flies that settled in banks upon the walls, whence the firemen washed them off with their jets. There were rats in their hundreds. And the residue of burned wheat was "a sticky mess that pulls your boots off".

There was a quite fantastic quantity of timber stored in the docks, much of it cut from extremely inflammable conifers and some loaded on to barges. These blazing barges were, when possible, cut loose from their moorings and went swinging down the river, only to return, still blazing, on the next tide. The chaos was enormous.

It must not be imagined that the docks were simply great areas of

warehouses and wharf and water guarded by night watchmen and fought for by firemen. Many people lived in and among them. Between the Surrey Docks and the river, and again on the north bank, in Silvertown, between the Victoria Docks and the Thames, there were narrow settlement of houses, missions and pubs. The people who lived in these now found themselves surrounded by fire, while the bombs poured down on them from the roaring sky.

In Bermondsey the inhabited strip between the Surrey Commercial Docks and the river is known locally as 'down town'. One main street, Rotherhithe Street, circles the blunt peninsula, with a number of short, narrow lanes running off it, and one road, Redriff Road, cuts through the acres of dock from the 'mainland' to join Rotherhithe Street. There are thus three bridges connecting 'down town' with the great sprawling mass of factories, back-to-back cottages and grimy goods yards that was

Bermondsey. When the docks blazed, the people were evacuated from down town and many of them were taken to Keeton's Road School. This building was not an air raid shelter and was in no way prepared as a reception centre. But after all, they had to be taken somewhere. A few hours later this school itself was bombed, and many people were killed.

Mr O'Connell was also a Post Warden, of L Post, actually out on Rotherhithe Street. He had been told, before the bombing started, that his was No. 1 Danger Zone, and this was certainly no exaggeration. He was a full-time warden and was on duty that night. This is his description of that night. 'Our first big fire was at Bellamy's Wharf and following that was one near the Surrey Lock Bridge, which we did our best to try and put out, and we did to a certain extent,

Air raid wardens, the heroes of the Blitz, receive elementary weapon training from a Home Guard officer

In Britain's pathetic shortage of weapons, some Home Guard units drilled with wooden sticks

and then we followed on with the break of a spell, and then we had the Dixon Street flare up, and that was a terrific fire, and all the personnel in that street did a magnificent job trying to get the incendiaries and everything out. Two firemen who were badly hurt in the fire were brought into my post, where I had to change all their clothes and give them two suits of overalls, and let them warm themselves because they were soaking with oil. And then Capsull's the paint factory, that went up in the air. We all had an order to watch out for parachutists coming down in the area.' This must have been almost exactly the hour when the Chiefs of Staffs were issuing code-word 'Cromwell'. 'And this certain thing was coming down which we thought all the time was a parachutist, but it happened to be a mine, which fell partly in the dock and set fire to the paint wells, and then we had Bellamy's Wharf, the egg warehouse. Well, Bellamy's Wharf, as we know, we had a vast lot of people under a shelter there, and also in Globe Wharf. I had a tidy few people in there, and in this shelter this night the top of it was well alight. And I called one of my individuals out on the quiet, and I says to him, I said – Bill, we shall have to evacuate the people out of this place. And with that I brought all the people out, even in our own dust carts.' Some of these were the people who were taken to the Keeton's Road School. Meanwhile the raid went on. To add to the problems of the night there were now delayed action bombs lying about, and at least one of these went off in Mr O'Connell's area. 'Things quietened down a bit after that, and then we had another big fire. And we had a bargeload of very burnable stuff, which was alcohol, and we had to cut that barge a-loose in the river. And then the dock itself was one mass of flame, and the barges of timber

The Home Guard at drill. Winston Churchill coined the name which appealed strongly to British sentiment

which my people cut loose from the sides of the wharves, to save the other timber, but I think it was labour in vain as far as that went.'

And so the night went on. Up at the far end of the Spa Road, Bermondsey, in the public baths, there was a casualty station. For the doctors and nurses, too, this was the night when the training of all the past quiet months was now put to the test. Dr Morton, a woman doctor at the baths, has described one of the surprises of that night and the following months:

'When we were training the first-aid workers, we took a great deal of time explaining how they should be aseptic: how they should scrub their hands before touching any wounds, how they should take care of asepsis when putting dressings on. But the very first night of the blitz that just went by the wind. What struck one was the tremendous amount of dirt and dust, the dirt and dust of ages blown up in every incident. Everyone came in looking absolutely filthy. Their heads were full of grit and dust, their skin was engrained with dust, and it was completely impossible to do anything much about anti-sepsis at all.' Yet, much to her surprise, almost no sepsis occurred in any of the cases that she followed up. It was all very rough and ready. 'In the Bermondsey baths, where we had our first-aid post, some of the bath attendants were using hose pipes to wash the people down. This cleaned their hair and gave them a good shampoo before we got going, and very grateful they were to get the grit out of their hair and their ears and their noses and so on.'

On the evening of 7th September , Police Sergeant Peters was helping with the rescue work. Here is his story:

'The first major incident to which I attended was at Keeton's Road School. The people had been evacuated from Rotherhithe owing to the docks being well on fire, and some were taken into Keeton's Road School along with all their belongings and their families

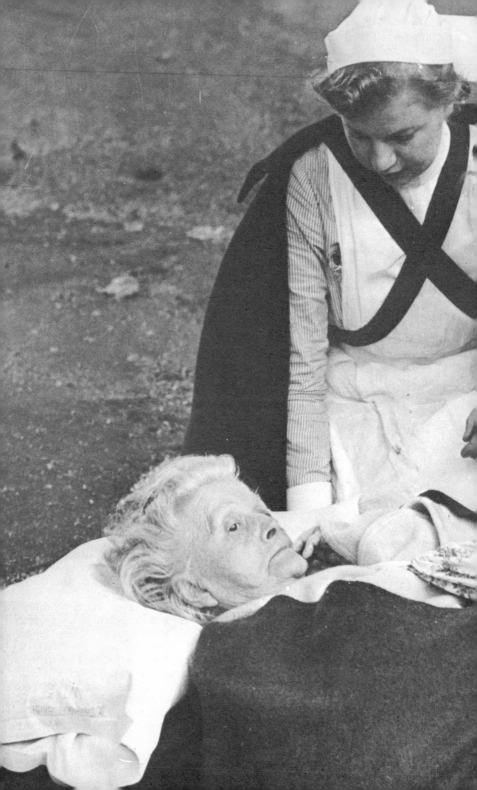

Evacuation for the old and infirm

and food. Soon after ten o'clock a bomb fell on the school and I, along with a number of others, was ordered down. On reaching the school we entered by the playground. Fire had started going through some of the rooms. In one room I saw an AFS man lying on a makeshift bedstead, and his face looked as if it had been skinned. A little further along I, with another officer, was searching amongst the debris and after a while my brother officer bent down and pulled something out. He thought it was a piece of bread. But it turned out to be part of a small child, the upper part, the upper limbs of a small child. This so upset us that we came out into the street. There were a number of bodies laying on the footway and in the road. I stood and watched these for a few moments. Eventually some of them stood up, and to my relief they were not all dead. But there were some of them who were dead.'

Thus did the Blitz come to Bermondsey. It was much the same in the neighbouring boroughs of Southwark and Deptford, Greenwich and Woolwich, and north of the river in Stepney, Poplar, West and East Ham.

In Poplar, for instance, Mr Cotter, who was Deputy Chief Warden of the borough, has written:

'First, let it be said at once that it has been impossible to compile a complete record of the bombs dropped on the borough on that afternoon and night of 7th September and the morning hours of 8th September. In twelve hours, twenty-two of our thirty-five telephones were put out of action with the result that wardens were only reporting casualty-producing incidents either by runner or over some odd telephone that happened to be working. For instance, a stick of six bombs would fall in a Post area, two of them causing casualties and the other four creating more or less serious damage. Almost invariably, the warden confined his reports to the casualty incidents, with a mental promise to compile a

complete list of other damage in the morning. Unfortunately, Sunday, 8th September brought a continuation of enemy activity and the mental promise was never put into effect. Throughout the first week or ten days, everyone was occupied with the task of locating and getting casualties to hospital; it was, I think, natural that many of the missiles were missed when a check-up was eventually put in hand. In addition, quite one-third of our members were themselves in difficulties; relatives had been killed or injured, homes had been totally demolished or so badly blasted that they were unfit for further habitation and alternative accommodation had to be found at once for wives and families. At ten or a dozen Posts, wardens were sleeping in chairs, cooking scratch meals and generally living a hand-to-mouth existence. All around them they saw friends and neighbours packing and preparing to move off into safe areas; never knowing what was to come, they decided, with very few exceptions, to stick and do their job.

'7th September and 132 Incidents – a

Anti-invasion watch on the south coast

single night's bombing which reached the total suffered by more fortunate areas in five years of the war. When, on the lines quoted above, one reckons the bombs which were not reported, the multitude of incendiary bombs, the missiles falling inside the dock enclosures, and the number of bombs dropped in the huge Devas Street fire, the total for this area of some 2½ square miles must have reached the saturation point for the whole of London. From all outlying parts of the metropolis, eyes were turned towards that Devas Street conflagration (the Dockside Fire) and tens of thousands of people wondered what was happening. They could not see stick after stick of bombs dropping into the flames and hurling burning wood, embers and showers of sparks hundreds of feet into the air; they could not see gangs of ARP workers clearing earth from buried Anderson shelters and bringing the occupants, dazed and half-suffocated, out into the revivifying air which was, none the less, heavy with smoke and redolent of charred timber; they could not visualise wardens picking their way through debris and, since phones had gone, making their way hurriedly to Control to report fresh incidents; they could not imagine the AFS crews, many of them literally receiving their baptism of fire, being hurled away from the blaze with hose and branches still gripped grimly in their hands; they could not see the Control staffs, perspiring, exhausted, foodless, endlessly ordering out fresh parties, nor could they hear the gasp of the telephone girl taking the air-raid message dealing with her own home.

'It would be impossible to relate fully the accounts of bravery and devotion to duty of members of all the Civil Defence services. Most of them were seeing violent death and wholesale destruction for the first time. At the rate missiles were falling and in view of the number of casualties on every side, there could have been no-one who, at some time or another during that first night, did not estimate his or her own chances of survival, and the obvious conclusion

Above: Women of London ambulance unit use their time between calls to make camouflage netting. *Below:* The stirrup pump, not very powerful, but often effective against small fires caught early. *Above right:* Operations Room at Fighter Command, the brain of Britain's fighter defences

would be that their chances were pretty slim.

'In one way, our task was tremendously simplified by the exodus on 7th September and during the succeeding weeks. At 7 pm on the first day, during an 'all clear' period, a positive convoy of motor vehicles, filled with entire families and piled high with luggage, rolled from side streets towards Bow Road and East India Dock Road and proceeded westwards. Some were proceeding to friends in the more fortunate London boroughs, while others were definitely on their way to the country for the duration. During the first few days, every available means of transport was used to remove the essentials for making a home elsewhere – crockery, pots and pans, and a few articles of furniture. Pony carts, hand-drawn barrows, perambulators and cycles with heavily laden carriers, all rolled out of the borough in a steady stream. At the Metropolitan Tube Station and at almost every bus stop, families burdened with suitcases and packages could be seen making their way out of the danger area; many of them no longer had a home and all they carried was the clothes in which they stood with perhaps an odd item or two salvaged from the wreckage.'

Poplar was a well-administered borough. Alderman Key, later the Regional Commissioner for Shelters, had organised the ARP services with outstanding efficiency. It was also particularly fortunate in possessing as Chief Warden E H Smith, later also Poplar's Mayor and a winner of the George Cross. The writer has been told that it was Smith and Cotter who kept Poplar going during these terrible first weeks. They were out, all night and every night, visiting almost every shelter, present at almost every incident, an example to the other wardens and a visible sign to the public of Poplar that they were neither forgotten nor neglected. There were others, of course, clergymen, doctors, the officers of the municipal administration and in particular the Town Clerk and his deputy. But Smith and Cotter were the men whom the people saw, and that tough and reliable pair kept Poplar's spirit from flagging. Alderman Smith was a Poplar man born and bred: he spoke the people's language, shares their political views, which are well to the left of centre, but more important perhaps was, quite obviously and at first glance, a leader. He had been a regular soldier for many years, starting as a drummer boy, and had the rare distinction of being awarded a battlefield commission in 1916. Cotter, a quietly-spoken and modest-mannered Irishman, a former officer of the Munster Fusiliers, was perhaps the ideal deputy for the rough-and-ready Smith. These two were Poplar, in 1940.

And the organisation, the ARP service, that bore the imprint of their characters was in some ways a unique one. For one thing, it was entirely democratic. The West End and residential boroughs had a wealth of potential or actual leaders on which to draw for their Wardens' services. Poplar did not. Therefore they decided that the Post Wardens should be elected, not appointed. And this was done, by the people of Poplar, from 1939 on. In each post area, the warden responsible for the people's safety and protection was those people's own choice. During the Blitz the percentage of votes cast in these elections was far greater than in any municipal or general election before or since. Much was written during that war about the defence of democracy. Alderman Smith's ARP service was a true example of democracy defending itself.

And the men and women elected by their neighbours and friends to the dangerous honour of patrolling the streets and controlling the incidents – the quaintly bureaucratic word invented to describe every sort of

Dornier 17s over the Thames on their way to the first attack

46

disaster inflicted by the enemy on the civilian population – were very conscious of the distinction that they had received and of the close scrutiny to which their behaviour was subjected.

Mr Cotter has described the attitude of the Wardens to their job, and to one another, in these words. (It should be said that one of the unwritten laws was that a Warden should not take shelter. He might, of course, go to an Anderson when off duty, or seek momentary safety from a stick of bombs in a brick street shelter, but the big shelters and the tubes were not for him.)

'What kind of people were our wardens? In Poplar we had a very rough-and-ready crowd indeed. If they liked you they probably called you "mate" irrespective of your rank; if they thought you were just passable they'd call you "mister", and if they disliked you they usually called you "sir". There was only one thing kept 'em together – they had a kind of discipline imposed by themselves, and that was the fear that their mates wouldn't think that a man was doing the job – they were afraid of their mates, definitely. We had one rather tragic case of a warden, a good one too, indeed, who was by chance seen in a tube shelter one night. He was with his wife. He went back to the Post the following morning with his usual cheery greeting: everybody refused to talk to him. They even took his name off the roster in the Post, and he was promptly sent to Coventry. We had of course to transfer him to another Post. The sad part of that story was that the man would never had gone into a deep shelter by himself. But his wife insisted he go along with her. And married men will know what I mean. . .'

Poplar stood up to the tremendous ordeal of that first night. Its neighbour across the River Lea, West Ham, came near to cracking.

It is necessary to examine West Ham

briefly, for it was in some important respects an exceptional borough.

Owing to industrial development during the 1800s, much of West Ham consisted of slum housing. The northern end of the borough, around Romford Road, contained, and still contains, many residential areas, the homes of what are now called the managerial class. But the southern end, by the river, was very bad. Canning Town, north of the Victoria and Albert Docks, and Silvertown, between those docks and the river, were the worst. In 1940 it contained about 13,000 people living in an area of rather less than one square mile, much of which was occupied by factories. The houses lay in narrow,

AA guns firing, known as 'the barrage'

crowded strips between the docks and the factories, dingy and squalid, many of them lodging houses for seafaring men and their women. Silvertown was not only physically difficult of access, its inhabitants felt themselves in other, subtler ways cut off from the rest of West Ham with its cinemas and schools and parks. Silvertown was thrown back on its own very slender resources for entertainment and recreation. West Ham as a whole contained the highest number of pubs per population of any borough in southern England.

Being a county borough, and not part of the London County Council itself, it was in a stronger position to argue with London Region and the Home Office than were the metropolitan boroughs. Before the Blitz its council had taken full advantage of this state of affairs. Since 1916 it had been a confirmed Labour Borough – it had returned Keir Hardie, the first Independent Labour Party member, to the House of Commons in 1892 – and in 1940, fifty-seven of its sixty-four council members were Labour.

Many were pacifists, and thus had been reluctant to deal with ARP matters before the war, and even before the Blitz. Their chief interest appears to have been in arguing that whatever had to be done should be paid for by the central administration. This was against the Government's policy in ARP matters, but accorded

with West Ham's policy in all matters. Before the war 42.6 per cent of West Ham's income came from Government grants. The result was a partial deadlock. Nor, it seems, did West Ham, before the Blitz, throw up any local man of the calibre of Poplar's E H Smith. There was a great shortage of Wardens. In one district, only four Wardens were less than forty years old, the remainder having an average age of sixty.

The missions and settlements did what they could, and the ARP arrangements at the factories were far superior to those of the borough. But there were almost no full-time voluntary workers. For this the Council was largely responsible. It had had a violent reaction from its pacifist past, and now refused to employ pacifists in any of its ARP services, thus depriving its people of the services of young men who, in other boroughs, did much brave and excellent work in Civil Defence rather than join the forces. The Council went further, and refused to allow pacifist organisations, such as the Friends' Ambulance Unit or the International Voluntary Service for Peace, to function at all within the borough. The self-opinionated fuddy-duddies at the Town Hall even distrusted the Women's Voluntary Service. West Ham was, in fact, singularly ill-prepared for the horrors of 7th September. What it was like in Silvertown that night is described by Lord Ritchie Calder, who went there shortly after the height of the raid.

'I sought out my old friend, "The Guv'nor", the militant clergyman, the Rev W W Paton. I found his Presbyterian church in ruins. His pulpit still stood, but the roof and the front wall had gone. The streets all around were wrecked. They were poor "Dead End" streets, running down to the dock wall, but these heaps of rubble had once been homes which sheltered the families of the East London dockers – tough, decent folk who had deserved better conditions than they'd ever had in peace-time

and who were having the worst in war. Some of these battered wrecks of brick and rubble, with shabby furniture now kindling, had been the only homes which old pensioners had ever known. They had "married into them"; they had brought up their families in them; they had seen their children married out of them; and were eking out an ill-cared-for old age in them – when the bombers came.

'I found "The Guv'nor" at last. He was ashen grey with the anguish of the night. He had been out in the raids helping his people throughout the night. His lips trembled and his eyes filled with tears when he spoke of those of his friends who were dead, injured or missing. But his main concern was with the living. He was dashing round the streets seeking out the survivors whose homes had been wrecked.

'I went with him. We found many hundreds of them sheltering in a school in the heart of the bombed area. I took a good look at this school. From the first glance it seemed to me ominous of disaster.

'In the passages and the classrooms were mothers nursing their babies. There were blind, crippled, and aged people. There were piccaninnies, the children of negro firemen then at sea. There were youngsters whom I knew by name, like the red-headed impish "Charlie" Whole families were sitting in queues, perched on their pitiful baggage, waiting desperately for coaches to take them away from the terror of the bombs which had been raining down on them for two nights. Yes, for two nights! For the blitzkrieg had started in that fore-doomed corner on the Friday night before London had felt the full weight of it.

'The crowded people in the school included many families who had been bombed out already, on that first night. These unfortunate homeless people had been told to be ready for the coaches at three o'clock. Hours later the coaches had not arrived. "The Guv'nor" and I heard women, the mothers of young children, protesting with violence and with tears about the delay. Men were cursing the helpless local officials who knew only that the coaches were expected. "Where are we going?" "Can't we walk there?" "We'll take a bus!" "There's a lorry we can borrow!" The crowd clamoured for help, for information, for reassurance. But the harassed officials knew no answer other than the offer of a cup of tea.

'One mother complained that her children and been forbidden to play in the playground. The official could only say he was sorry and evade her questions. But he showed me the answer. In the playground behind the school was a crater. The school was, in fact, a bulging, dangerous ruin. The bombs which had rendered thése people homeless had also struck the school, selected by the authorities as their "Rest Centre". Note that the school had already been bombed at the same time as "The Guv'nor's" church had been bombed. So had the parish church which, because it was the favourite "church-wedding" place of the poor, was known as "The Cathedral of East London". So had other buildings and streets in a direct line with it. And then I knew, on that Sunday afternoon, that, as sure as night would follow the day, bombers would come again with the darkness, and that school would be bombed.

'It was not a premonition. It was a calculable certainty. These hapless people told me how the bombers had ranged over the Docks, shedding their bombs – one, two, three, four, then a pause as the 'planes banked in a tight turn and that remorseless fifth bomb, dropped each time on the same corner.

'All these hundreds of people spent another night inside the shelterless school. Some were taken to another school – providentially – although it was only the breadth of a street away! This was done to make room for a new flood of homeless victims of the

London blazes during the night after the first attack

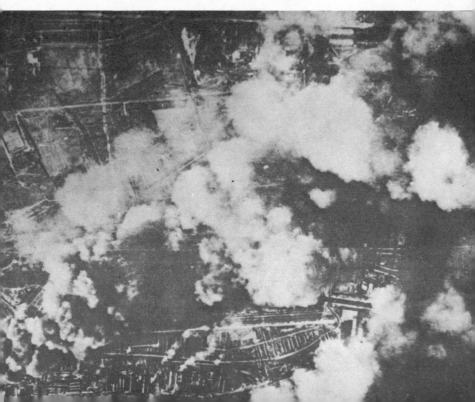

Sunday night raids. During yet another night of raids and terror, the fourth on the school for some of the shelterers, the inevitable bomb hit the crowded building.

'The next morning I saw the crater. I saw the rescue men descending perilously into it, with ropes around them, saw them pause, every now and then, in a hushed painful silence, listening for sounds of the living; saw the tomb of whole families of many of my "Dead End Kids". By then, two days after the coaches had been due, the survivors, mainly from that second school, were boarding buses. They were struggling for places as crowds clamber aboard at the rush-hour. I spoke to men, fathers of families, who had been cursing on the Sunday. They were speechless and numbed by the horror of it all now.

Dockland burns

They had been saved by the breadth of that road!

'An inquiry was started. It was found that the coaches had been ordered on the Sunday all right. The drivers had been told to rendezvous at "The George" public-house in a neighbouring borough. The leader of the convoy thought he knew "The George". He did, but it was "The George" in a different borough. So the coaches just went home. Next day,

coaches arrived at the school, but as the homeless were boarding them the sirens went. Local officials decided to abandon the transfer that day and attempt it the following day. The next day was too late.

'This tragedy was one of the first and grimmest lessons of London. About 450 homeless lost their lives in that school – a figure to be dismissed lightly by those who measure casualties in terms of Passchendaele or the

Somme. It was the needlessness of the tragedy which made it so terrible.'

West Ham was left a desolate, despairing ruin.

It was not easy to do anything for its embittered people, who revolted now without reason, even against measures designed for their own safety and comfort. Their attitude will become more apparent in the chapter about shelters. For outsiders, even if they could get past the senseless barriers erected by the West Ham Council, it was difficult in the extreme to help. Yet, despite all the rumours, there was no more panic than has been here described. There was bitterness, anger, even perhaps despair. But just as there were no leaders in West Ham to organise the defence of the borough before the Blitz – later the Rev W W Paton was compelled by force of circumstances to take effective control – so there was no one to canalise this sensation of abandonment and misery into the sort of mass uprisings which Hitler had hoped his bombing would produce.

The night raid had been carried out by some 250 bombers of Air Fleets Two and Three, and they had dropped about 330 tons of high explosive and 440 incendiary canisters on East London. Though these riverside boroughs suffered most, every part of London was hit, Victoria and London Bridge Stations so badly that they were closed for some days.

The Government communiqué said: 'Fires were caused among industrial targets. Damage was done to lighting and other public service, and some dislocation to communications was caused. Attacks have also been directed against the docks. Information as to casualties is not yet available.'

The people had learned by now to read subtleties of meaning into the strangely laconic and non-committal prose of these official announcements.

Junkers 88s are lined up before an operation

Everyone realised at once that a very heavy and murderous raid had taken place. Between five o'clock on the evening of 7th September and three o'clock the following morning, the German bombers had killed about one thousand Londoners or over 5 per cent of London's total casualties throughout the Blitz. During the night raid, no enemy plane was shot down.

That evening Göring addressed the German nation over the wireless, even while his night bombers were setting out again for London. Amid threats and boasts and promises, he said:

'This is the historic hour when for the first time our air force delivered its thrust right into the enemy's heart.'

But if London is the heart of Britain and the Commonwealth, and was then, perhaps, the heart of all western civilisation, where is London's heart? The docks were damaged, and much was burned, but they were not put out of action to any great extent. And in any case, can they be called London's heart? Or is it perhaps to be found in Whitehall, or St Paul's, or Piccadilly Circus, or the Elephant and Castle, or Buckingham Palace, or Oxford Street, or the House of Commons? Each of these was to be struck in turn in the weeks to come and London's heart, though it might seem to miss a beat – as it did on this first night – continued to pump the blood of resolution through the arteries of Britain and the free world.

Göring's metaphor was wrong. He had not struck at the heart, but rather at the hide of this great, grey city which sprawls, shapeless as a whale, about its river. His darts had hurt. The pachyderm had winced and shifted. But what had he achieved? A child dismembered in Bermondsey, a timber fire in Poplar, a plague of flies in West Ham, a blazing gas pipe in Chelsea. Multiply that a thousand times, and it is still not a great wound, let alone a mortal one, to a city the size of London. But it was a wound.

The morning after

The next day, Sunday 8th September, had already been appointed a day of national prayer. It was also a day of extreme tension, rumour and activity. The issuing of the code-word 'Cromwell' on the evening before had led many people to believe that the invasion had actually begun. In some of the eastern counties soldiers blocked the roads, and the Home Guard sounded the tocsin by ringing the church bells. Stories were soon on everyone's lips of German bodies washed ashore on the Isle of Wight, of the sea being set ablaze by the RAF, of a great naval battle fought in the Straits of Dover. As a topic of conversation in the country lanes, on the way back from matins that morning, the invasion that had not happened was a keen competitor of the Blitz that had. Human imagination, when totally unfettered by reality, can always well outbid the truth.

In London, at least outside the stricken boroughs, rumour also had a great day. The authorities were naturally anxious to prevent sightseers and other curious individuals from entering the docks area, and these were at once sealed off by the police, while the firemen continued to fight the conflagrations – which were all under control by the time darkness fell – and the Civil Defence organisations attempted to deal with the first, monumental chaos. Luckily enough, though the sun was shining over London, there was considerable low cloud over the French coast. This, combined presumably with the normal needs for rest and overhaul of the German crews and their planes, was responsible for the fact that there was no daylight raid on London that Sunday, though a number of enemy bombers were over the southern counties.

During the day it soon became apparent that although the damage to warehouses, and to the streets behind the docks, was very great, the docks themselves were not mortally hit. The German newspapers announced hopefully that London was no longer a seaport. This was quite untrue. London, even throughout these next few weeks, continued to be the world's busiest, as it was the world's largest, port. It is one thing to burn huge stacks of timber and other commodities in the dock area: it is quite another to put the dock installations themselves out of action. And the great proportion of the docks remained at all times open and working.

But if the docks were to continue to function, there must be dockers to unload the ships. And those dockers must themselves have somewhere to live. It was the damage to property that confronted the authorities with their immediate biggest problem once the fires were under control. Those authorities had of course realised that many houses would be destroyed by the enemy's bombs, but they had simultaneously over-estimated to a

The homeless salvage their belongings from the wreckage

Above: A bomb victim is rescued from the rubble. *Below:* Cockney spirits remain high despite the damage

fantastic extent the number of people who would be killed or so badly hurt that they must go to hospital. They had, apparently, more or less equated the two, and it was roughly assumed that the amount of houses left standing after the bombers had gone would contain enough living space to house the survivors. It was of course realised that this would not take place entirely automatically, but only the sketchiest arrangements were made.

In the first place the problem of dealing with the homeless was handed over to the boroughs and made the responsibility of the poor law authorities. Their directives laid down that they were to organise feeding stations and temporary shelters of some kind for the homeless. They were not entitled to requisition buildings for this purpose: they were expected only to look after the homeless citizens of their own boroughs: they were not encouraged to look after them for long: and they received almost no financial or other special assistance from the central Government in carrying out these instructions. Supplies of such items as blankets, stocks of food, crockery and so on were either non-existent or inadequate. The theory behind this apparently callous policy, or absence of policy, was based on the general misapprehension of what the raids would be like.

It was hoped that after the sharp, short raids, probably by day, that were anticipated, the homeless – after a brief visit to a rest centre where they would be given a cup of tea, identity papers if theirs had been destroyed, and perhaps a minimum of financial assistance – would either go back to their bombed homes and put them in order, or would find alternative accommodation for themselves with friends or relatives. A Government circular stated that 'a small residuum' might have to be officially billeted. It was believed that these people would only be in the rest centres for a few hours. There was therefore no need to make such centres comfortable, sanitary, or, apparently, even safe. Indeed it was considered wiser not to do so, since this might make the people want to stay in places that were intended for no such purpose. The result, of course, was that when the bombing began the homeless were taken to buildings like the Keeton's Road School and the school in West Ham described in the previous chapter.

The question of voluntary evacuation was even more intractable in view of the Government's directives to the boroughs, and the psychological background created by the failed evacuation of 1939. Homeless, shocked, penniless people might – and did – pour out of the bombed boroughs, but they were not anyone else's responsibility. The poor law authorities, inevitably not the most open-handed of men, could hardly be expected to devote their inadequate stocks of food and clothing to destitute strangers, when their own people were likely to be in the same condition within days or even hours.

This problem of the homeless, the bombed-out, was to affect large parts of London and many of the great provincial cities in the weeks and months to come. But it appeared in its most acute form immediately, on 8th September and during the next twenty days in the East End riverside boroughs.

What was to be done with them? A proportion fled, in any conveyance or even on foot, from the next night's terror. Five thousand are said to have trecked out nightly into Epping Forest where they slept in the open air and, regrettably enough, were occasionally treated as felons by the lucky inhabitants of the respectable adjoining suburbs. Many spent the night on Hampstead Heath or in Greenwich Park. Others went even further afield. For nearly two months several hundred 'unauthorised evacuees' were living in the Majestic Cinema in Oxford, eating, sleeping and, to the disgust of the burghers of that ancient and unbombed centre of learning, even copulating among the cinema seats. A visitor to one such cinema – it may have been the same one – described it in a contemporary Mass Observation bulletin as follows:

'I slept the night in the cinema. It is lit by six large lights; four of these are turned off at eleven o'clock, the other two remain on all night. Firemen and nurses patrol the cinema throughout the night, the nurses tucking up children, fetching water and milk, and so on. Each family takes a small piece of ground as their own province. Some are in the orchestra pit, and are given a little privacy by the curtains in front of it. But the majority sleep in the gangways and between the seats There are perhaps 800 in all in the cinema. All are provided with blankets and palliasses. These they park somewhere and put their belongings (mostly a change of clothing) on the seats nearby. When it is bedtime the men take off their coats, the women their overalls, and lie down. The gangways become crowded, people lying very close to one another. Between the seats there is perhaps an average of one person to a row of ten seats. Here and there is a baby in his pram. There is no noise during the night, except of babies crying. Nearly every mother has a small child, and as soon as one cries, three or four others start too. It was quite impossible to get more than ten minutes uninterrupted sleep.'

But a person named Lady Patricia Ward, who wrote in a national newspaper, seems to have worn spectacles of another colour when visiting this cinema:

'The East End loved it. They settled themselves down each night, on rugs and cushions and blankets along the

Below: The firemen fight a losing battle against fires which burned on a scale never previously encountered. *Right:* Gutted buildings in the last stages of the blaze

corridors; in the daytime they sat in the tip-up seats and sent their children to play in a disused ice-rink at the back of the stage . . . and wasn't it a lovely, bright place, almost like a palace? So they told each other.'

It is not hard to imagine what some of these unfortunate people may have told each other, if they happened to read Lady Patricia's article.

There were tens of thousands of these unfortunate refugees roaming the countryside. By 14th September almost a quarter of the population of some badly hit boroughs had gone. Reception arrangements in the country were inadequate or non-existent. One country rest centre greeted the bombed-out with a large notice, stating: 'Behind every social problem is revealed the hidden hand of alcohol'. Profiteering was rife. Sixteen guineas a week was demanded and obtained for a Cotswold cottage, eighteen shillings for a tiny bedroom

in Hertfordshire, eight-and-six for a wretched dinner at a West Country hotel, and money then was worth more than thrice what it is today. It was not until September 18th that the Ministry of Health took preliminary steps to meet the conditions that had arisen, and to organise this new evacuation or flight. On 24th September mothers with children of school age were declared eligible for evacuation, under the state scheme, from eight of the worst-hit boroughs: on 7th October this was extended to all the County of London. But on 1st November there were still over 250,000 children in the capital.

Attempts had been made to find the bombed-out alternative places to live in the city itself. For example, on 9th September the town clerk of Stepney, on his own initiative, arranged that a thousand or so people be evacuated by river steamer from Wapping to Richmond and other

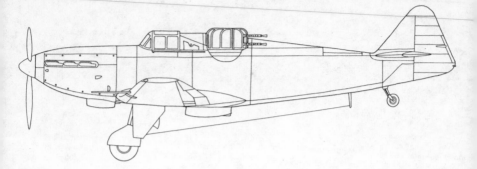

The Boulton Paul Defiant was conceived as a day fighter with all its armament concentrated in a power driven turret, which was thought for a time to be more efficient than fixed guns. But after some initial success in combat, the Defiant began to prove an easy victim for the more nimble and heavily armed conventional German fighters, and was therefore relegated to night fighter duties. It was later fitted with radar, but the fighter was never more than a stopgap in this role. *Crew*: 2. *Engine*: Rolls Royce Merlin III, 1,030 hp. *Armament*: four .303-inch Browning machine guns with 600rpg. *Speed*: 304mph at 17,000 feet. *Range*: 465 miles. *Ceiling*: 30,350 feet. *Weight empty/loaded*: 6,078/8,600 pounds. *Span*: 39 feet 4 inches. *Length*: 35 feet 4 inches

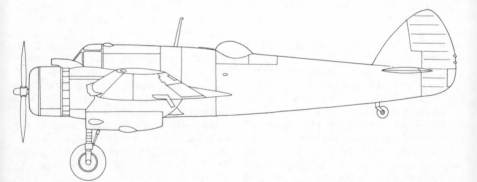

The Bristol Beaufighter was one of Britain's most successful night fighters during the course of the war. Developed as a fighter variant of the Beaufort torpedo bomber, the Beaufighter was rushed into production with early AI radar, a Beaufighter making its first kill on November 11, 1940. *Crew*: 2. *Engines*: Two Bristol Hercules XI radials, 1,590 hp. *Armament*: four 20mm Hispano cannon with 240 rpg and six .5-inch Browning machine guns with 1,000 rpg. *Speed*: 323mph at 15,000 feet. *Range*: 1,500 miles. *Ceiling*: 28,900 feet. *Climb*: 1,850 feet per minute. *Weight empty/loaded*: 14,069/20,800 pounds. *Span*: 57 feet 10 inches. *Length*: 41 feet 4 inches towns up-stream which had agreed to find them billets. On 11th September the Minister of Health, Mr Malcolm Macdonald, promised that on the following day buses would be sent to Silvertown and all who wished to leave that desolate place, whether homeless or not, could do so. In fact only 2,900 persons, out of an original population of some 14,000, accepted this offer which they had been assured would not be repeated.

West End billets for these people were not very popular. They believed that they would be treated as pariahs, and on occasions they were. For example, a rich family in Belgravia, with a large house, had a bombed-out family from Whitechapel billeted on them. The rich put the poor in the servants' quarters – that it to say, under the eaves and nearest to the bombers – and refused to let them shelter in the basement where they themselves slept. The refugees preferred to return to Whitechapel. Such cruelty was undoubtedly the exception but tales of this sort travel fast. They travelled extremely fast in the East End, and once the full measure of the terror had been faced most of the inhabitants of those boroughs who were still there preferred, whenever possible, to remain among their own battered, broken streets, even though their homes had gone. But where were they to sleep and eat and wash? That was the problem that had to be faced on 8th September.

The homeless were not only those whose homes had been destroyed, but also the people who were forced to leave their houses or flats because an unexploded bomb (UXB) had landed nearby.

To begin with it was ordered that all premises within six hundred yards of such a bomb must be immediately evacuated and the roads within this area closed. This turned out to be quite impractical. A few hundred UXBs, skilfully placed, would have put all central London out of action, and by late November there were no

less than 3,000 of these unpleasant objects waiting to be dealt with in London Region alone. Nevertheless, though decreasing the danger zone, the Government continued with its policy whereby all UXBs were to be regarded as delayed-action bombs. From a purely military point of view it would undoubtedly have been wiser to treat them all as duds, unless they were actually ticking, and risk the very occasional explosion. The saving in time and in trouble caused by evacuation and traffic diversions would have been enormous. On the other hand the people might then have complained that they were not being properly protected.

In any event the Government's decision concerning these nuisances served vastly to increase the numbers of the homeless. Since people evacuated on account of UXBs expected soon to be able to return to their homes, they were naturally not very interested in finding alternative accommodation, even of a temporary sort. And since they were often ordered from their homes at the shortest notice, or prevented from entering them on their return from work or after a night in the shelters, they too often arrived at the Rest Centres as destitute as the truly bombed out. Finally, since the bomb disposal crews were quite hideously overworked, the temporarily evacuated were often a charge on the public assistance authorities for days on end. This was a major contributory cause to the congestion in the Rest Centres.

Professor Titmuss, in his official history entitled *Problems of Social Policy*, has a great deal to say about the conditions of those centres as they were in those early days.

They were usually in schools. The standard diet, provided for children as well as adults, consisted of bread, margarine, potted meat or corned beef, with an occasional bowl of tinned soup. There was frequently no crockery or cutlery. On 12th

Above: East Enders settle down to communal living. *Right:* Inside an air raid shelter

September one such centre in Bethnal Green had two spoons and a blunt knife. In another centre it was impossible to open the tins of soup because there was no tin-opener. There might be a few blankets, but usually no other bedding – or indeed beds – for the bombed-out, who often arrived wearing only their night-clothes. Sometimes there were not even enough chairs. In a previous chapter Dr Morton has described the all-enveloping filth that was thrown up by the bombs. The bombed-out were almost always extremely dirty, but most of the Rest Centres had inadequate washing facilities, or none at all. Sanitary conditions were little better. Some of the Rest Centres soon became quite disgusting.

A Red Cross worker described a particularly bad one in a report which she sent to Lord Horder at the time, and which he forwarded to the Ministry of Health. It had been an elementary school, in Stepney, and each September night the floor was crowded with some two or three hundred homeless people, lying on blankets, mattresses and piles of clothing. They had ten pails and coal-scuttles to use as lavatories. 'By the middle of the night these containers . . . overflow so that, as the night advances, urine and faeces spread in ever-increasing volume over the floor. The space is narrow, so that whoever enters inevitably steps in the sewage and carries it on his shoes all over the building . . . the containers are not emptied until 8 am. By dawn the stench . . . but I leave that to your imagination.' These people were provided with seven basins to wash in, but no soap or towels.

Another social worker, also quoted by Professor Titmuss, wrote as follows:

'The picture of the rest centres in those early days is unforgettable.

Dim figures in dejected heaps on unwashed floors in total darkness: harassed, bustling, but determinedly cheerful helpers distributing eternal corned beef sandwiches and tea – the London County Council panacea for hunger, shock, loss, misery and illness . . . Dishevelled, half-dressed people wandering between the bombed house and the rest centre salvaging bits and pieces, or trying to keep in touch with the scattered family . . . A clergyman appeared and wandered about aimlessly, and someone played the piano.'

Voluntary social workers soon arrived to do what they could, and they did a great deal. The various charitable organisations distributed large quantities of blankets, clothes and food, and those admirable women, the spiritual daughters of Florence Nightingale, who always appear at last to sort out the chaos when the male authorities have almost given up in despair, soon got to work. Many of these were not trained social workers, nor did they accept the rigid bureau-

cratic methods of the overwhelmed public assistance administrators. 'They raided school feeding centres and took away cutlery and crockery without permission, they bought food out of a variety of charitable funds, they appropriated babies' nappies and clothes . . . and one at least fetched to a centre administered by the public assistance committee coal which belonged to the local education committee.'

In West Ham, in those first days, there were no canteens, mobile canteens or communal feeding centres. In one Rest Centre there was no food available for a great many people save sardines, hard biscuits and meat roll. A pie-shop keeper, with the appropriate name of Cook, came to the rescue. His shop had been burned out, and with it all his cooking equipment. But he collected some old drainpipes, caulked them together with dough, and mended his oven. Next day he sold 2,700 dinners, consisting of celery soup, meat pie, potatoes and bread.

He charged 4d. per meal and not only fed the hungry but even made a profit for himself.

In Islington there was a red-faced, loud-voiced, middle-aged woman who for years had made her living selling beetroots from a barrow in the market. She simply marched into the Ritchie Street Rest Centre and took charge. She found milk for the babies, bedded them down with their mothers and gave them each a powder, the ingredients of which are lost to history. However, this powder sent them all quickly to sleep. She then gave the remaining beds and benches to the oldest and feeblest people there, and by the time that night's raid began her whole household, consisting of 103 persons, was asleep or dozing. In the morning she organised washing, bathed the babies, swept the floor, and supervised breakfast. She left at eleven, presumably to sell her beetroots. In the evening she returned. As Professor Titmuss has said: 'She made one rest centre a place of security, order and decency for hundreds of homeless people.'

And, of course, after a little while the Government and the LCC stepped in. The worst period was in middle and late September when the population of the Rest Centres rose to some 25,000. Thereafter the figures fell, billeting was properly organised, and the centres themselves, now made decent and run with tolerable efficiency, reverted to their intended role. People no longer lived in them, but simply went there for a meal, a wash, an issue of clothing if necessary, and above all advice.

But on 8th September it was to places such as those described above that the bombed-out, and those evacuated because of UXBs, had, in many cases, to go.

The British defences against the night bombing during the first phase of the Blitz were both slight and ineffective. There were two forms of active defence: the night fighters and the anti-aircraft guns.

The anti-aircraft gunners had long been the Cinderella of the army. After the First World War this branch of the service was scrapped altogether, and in 1920 the establishment of both AA guns and searchlights was nil. It was re-created, but it seemed a hopeless job. In 1926, during combined exercises with the RAF, guns, firing from permanent emplacements at targets flying on a known course, at a known speed, and at a height that was ideal for the gunners, scored only two hits out of 2,935 rounds fired. It is hardly surprising that the report on this fiasco stated that the chief effect of AA fire must 'still be regarded as mainly moral'. Only in 1934 was it again considered possible that AA guns might actually shoot down enemy planes. When it came to re-equipping the army in the 1930s, however, this dubious arm was very low on the priority list. In early 1938 the total AA defences of Great Britain consisted of 100 guns and 800 lights, when 216 guns and 1,056 lights were recognised as the minimum establishment for the defence of London alone. In October of 1939 General Pile, who had succeeded General Alan Brooke as GOC AA Command, some months earlier, spoke of his command's 'terrible inefficiency'

It was not only guns and searchlights that were in short supply. During the first year of the war AA Command got the dregs of the call-up. Out of twenty-five recruits sent to one battery, one had a withered arm, one was mentally deficient, one had no thumbs, one had a glass eye which fell out whenever he doubled to the guns, and two were in the advanced and more obvious stages of venereal disease. Out of 1,000 recruits sent to the 31st AA Brigade, fifty had to be discharged immediately, twenty more were mentally deficient, and a further eighteen were below medical category B2. Of the useful recruits many were young soldiers, too young to be sent overseas, who were not infrequently transferred to other branches of the

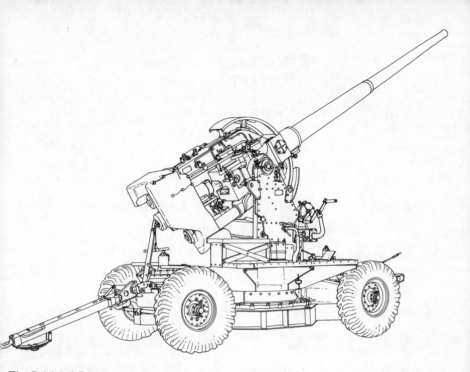

The British 4.5-inch anti-aircraft gun was designed for use against faster moving and higher aircraft, where the 3.7-inch gun was at a disadvantage. It fired a 55 pound shell with a muzzle velocity of 2,400 feet per second up to a maximum effective ceiling of 34,200 feet. Its normal rate of fire was eight rounds per minute

artillery once they were old enough and trained. Meanwhile the Command was drained of experienced officers and NCOs who were sent to the BEF. Many of these returned, *via* Dunkirk, but usually of course without their guns.

This was the Augean stable which General Pile had to put in order. When the bombing of London began, AA strength for the whole of Britain was approximately fifty per cent of the heavy and thirty-three per cent of the light guns as envisaged in the pre-war programme. Most of those guns, and the methods of firing them, were, according to Pile, 'technically entirely unfitted for dealing with any but the bomber of twenty years earlier'. Their fire was controlled by sound-locators and the Fixed Azimuth system. In London a complicated and expensive Fixed Azimuth apparatus had been installed before the war,

when it was realised that full radar defence would not be ready in time for the impending battle. 'Information from a geometrical layout of sound locators was passed through an ingenious computing apparatus in a central control room, and was from there conveyed to the guns. But it was based on our old assumption that the enemy would fly on a straight course and at a constant height and speed, and as the information depended on sound (with its consequent inaccuracy), and as the cumbersome machinery produced only a small volume of fire for a large number of guns, it failed lamentably.'

Furthermore, during the first few days of the Blitz, the gunners had to identify the planes as hostile before firing, since British night fighters were also operating over and about London.

The result of all this was that

during the nights of 7th, 8th and 9th September there was only the occasional banging of an anti-aircraft gun to be heard in London, an insignificant noise among the crash of bombs and the steady, broken drone of the bombers. Indeed, only ninety-two 'heavy' guns were in position when the Blitz started, and the German bombers flew usually above the ceiling of the lighter AA guns. The people, in their shelters or in the wretched Rest Centres, felt again that nothing was being done to protect them. During these three heavy raids only four enemy planes were shot down out of more than 600 bombers that had bombed London by night. By the night of 9th–10th September it seemed, not only to the public, that Anti-Aircraft Command was almost a total failure.

That night, General Pile says, 'it was obvious to me, sleeping in my bed, that our system was no good. I became both angry and frightened at the same time, and lay awake the rest of the night thinking how to deal with this business.'

Next day he held a conference and determined that, regardless of all previous theories, in the next night's raid he would fire off every gun he could at the enemy planes. He had been bringing in guns from the provinces and the ports for the last two days, and he now had 199 barrels at his disposal. Later that day he summoned the commanders of every gun position in London, together with their Battery Brigade and Divisional commanders, to the Signals Drill Hall in the Brompton Road, where he addressed them personally. He said that every gun was to fire every possible round. Fire was not to be withheld on any account. Guns were to be got to the approximate bearing and elevation, and then fired. RAF night fighters would not be operating over London and every plane was to be engaged immediately, without waiting to identify it. 'What in effect we were doing', he says, 'was to use our predictors, with all the information we could feed into them from any source, to engage the enemy by predicted

Above left: The effects of blast strong enough to lift a London bus. *Above:* An Anderson shelter which saved a family's lives, despite being badly damaged in an almost direct hit. *Below:* Street trade goes on as usual

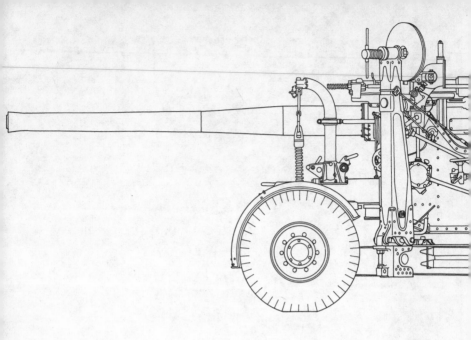

The 3.7-inch Anti-Aircraft Gun Mark I was the basic British anti-aircraft gun, possessing characteristics very similar to the dreaded German '88' – the 88mm anti-aircraft gun. With guns of this relatively light calibre, mobility was an important prerequisite, hence the four large wheels. These were raised when the gun was about to go into action, while four arms with adjustable pads were lowered to take their place and hold the gun level when firing. It was an extremely good and versatile gun. Crew varied between nine and eleven, and its maximum effective range was about 11,000 yards

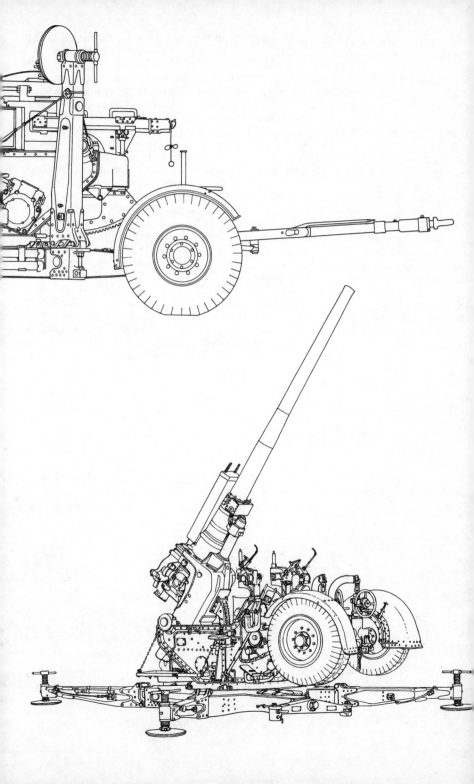

fire from all the guns that could bear on any particular target. It was in no sense a barrage, though I think by that name it will always be known.'

That night the barrage opened up, and its roar was music in the ears of the Londoners. The results astonished Pile, the London public and apparently the German pilots too, who flew higher as the night went on. Many of them, seeing the twinkling shell-bursts in the sky ahead, jettisoned their bombs on the southern and eastern suburbs and turned for home.

This new method of firing was scarcely more effective in destroying enemy planes than the old had been, and until the arrival of radar sets on the gun sites very few night bombers were shot down. But as a morale-booster for the people on the ground, its effect was incalculable. Though it is certain that during these first weeks ack-ack shells and shell fragments killed many more English civilians

The Observer Corps in action, keeping track of all aircraft, hostile and allied, which enter and leave Britain

than German airmen, the noise of the guns not only went some way to drowning the noises made by the enemy, but also gave Londoners the impression that their own people were hitting back at last. They even, rather touchingly, collected the lethal white-hot shell fragments which throughout that winter clattered and sparked into their streets. These lumps of gashed steel are still to be seen on many a mantelpiece.

So far as the Germans went, the very fact that the sky was full of bursting shells strongly discouraged the bomber crews from pin-pointing their targets. The consequent dispersal was of course very much in the interests of the defence. The Civil Defence services of individual boroughs were not swamped by concentrated attack, for the suffering and damage was more widely, which means more thinly, spread.

Those experts who had said, fourteen years before, that anti-aircraft fire was primarily concerned with morale were proved to have prophesied with a curious accuracy, at least so far as the

night raids of these first few weeks went.

There was, as usual, the delightful eccentric who objected. The council of one suburban borough wrote complaining that the vibration of the guns was cracking the lavatory pans of the council houses, and would AA Command please be so good as to move its barrage elsewhere? While a gentleman sent a letter to General Pile saying: 'Dear Sir, As a citizen of London, I think the anti-aircraft defence of London is the biggest scandal since Nero . . . Why, you don't understand the meaning of the word barrage . . .'

The strain on the gunners was very great. Many of them were raw recruits, living in crude dugouts they themselves had built beside their gun-sites, often deep in mud, often half-full of water and half demolished by the blast of gun and bomb. One battery arrived from the Midlands twenty-four hours after receiving its movement order and was firing within three quarters of an hour of being ready for action. For ten hours they served the guns. They then boiled them out. They had half an hour's sleep before the day raid began, and the same men took post again. This went on for eight days, at the end of which time they were almost unconscious at their guns for lack of sleep. On the ninth day they were relieved by soldiers who had had no more than basic training.

The guns, too, suffered. The gun barrels were wearing out, and twice Pile attempted to cut down on the firing. But Churchill immediately noticed the decrease in the nightly din, and that most sensitive politician knew exactly what the barrage meant to the population of London. He telephoned through at once to demand why all the guns were not firing. They fired, and they went on firing so long as the intensive Blitz on London continued, even though General Pile reckoned in late October that at this rate he would have no 4·5s left in two months and no 3.7s in four. But by then the Blitz was about to move elsewhere.

Night fighters, in those early days, were even less successful than the anti-aircraft gunners. Group-Captain John Cunningham was to be the most successful night-fighter ace. Before the winter was out he, usually with Squadron-Leader Rawnsley, his navigator, was to shoot down more than a dozen enemy bombers. But all that came later. He has described the acute frustation of those early weeks, to this writer, in these words:

'The September to November period was the most depressing for night fighters. We had mainly Blenheims in our squadrons then.' On 7th September there were, in Southern England or the Midlands, five squadrons of Blenheims, a flight of night-fighter Hurricanes and another of Defiants. 'The Blenheims had a very inadequate form of radar. Most nights we were able to hear the aircraft going over our airfields before we got into the aeroplanes to take off. But having started up, and got into the air, we were seldom if ever able to see them. The radar wasn't working well enough to enable us to get contacts and close in that way. On the very few occasions when the searchlights did illuminate the enemy aircraft, you were usually in the wrong place or not high enough, and by the time you got near the target the searchlight would have gone off it, or the aeroplane would have flown away from the searchlight region. So one was left with a feeling of almost complete helplessness. But in October the first Beaufighters arrived in squadron . . .'

The story of the radar-directed night fighter belongs later in this book.

While awaiting the arrival of the new night fighters and above all of the new airborne radar sets and ground installations which would enable the night fighters to close with the enemy, many expedients were tried, all without success. One was the use of single-seater day fighters by night. This proved both expensive, owing to the number that crashed on landing, and unsuccessful, though a few kills were recorded on the rare occasions when the moon and cloud produced an almost daytime clarity. But every single day fighter, and its pilot, was needed for the day battle, at least during the first weeks. This experiment was soon abandoned. Others were tried. Squadron-Leader Rawnsley, in his book *Night Fighter*, has written:

'The authorities tried all kinds of ingenious and even fantastic schemes, and a vast amount of thought and effort was expended on a fallacy. We now knew where the solution lay; but how could we, on our past showing, expect them to put all their eggs in one black and as yet unproved basket?

'The fallacy lay in their deep-rooted and understandable conviction that our failure was due simply to our inability to see another aircraft in the dark. We knew well enough that there would be no difficulty about that if – and this was the important point – we could be brought into the right position relative to the aircraft we were pursuing, going at the same speed and in the same direction. But first of all we had to be placed in the right position to make full use of our own radar.

'But other schemes were brought into play and we were beset with such things as airborne searchlights, showers of magnesium flares, airsown minefields dangling on parachutes, and other menaces to our own defensive fighters. Some of these schemes were good enough in theory, but the practical difficulties were too great. And they all missed the most essential point of all: to get the fighter into a position where it could make an attack.

'It was said of one very new pilot on one of his first night patrols that he

The bombing was not confined to the East End dockland. This attack severely damaged Oxford Street in the West End

suddenly saw an airborne searchlight projected horizontally out of the darkness at his own level without knowing what it was. He immediately lost all faith in his instruments and dived straight into the ground!

'Another source of amusement for us was the correspondence columns of the more irresponsible newspapers. There we read of people who wanted anti-aircraft guns mounted on balloons; of the idea that bombers should fly above the raiders and drop sand into their engines; and there was even one who suggested forming up a hundred obsolete aircraft in line astern, each trailing a thousand feet of cable, to fly across the track of the raider'.

'Fortunately for all of us the sponsors of the radar-equipped night fighter were not side-tracked."

The night-fighter pilots did not, at this time, enjoy the immense prestige and popularity that the Spitfire and Hurricane pilots won in the Battle of Britain, and that they themselves were to acquire in the coming months. Squadron-Leader Rawnsley has told this writer the following anecdote of the period:

'I'm afraid we weren't very proud of our performance in those early days. We had the feeling that we weren't doing our stuff, that we were letting the public down. And most of us were Londoners. When we went home on forty-eight hour leave occasionally, we were only too glad to get back to the comparative safety of the aerodrome. I remember one of our airgunners who went home and went to his local pub. They were giving him a good time on the strength of his Air Force uniform when he inadvisedly let drop the information that he was not in bombers but in night fighters. He was immediately met with the rejoinder: Oh, you are, are you? And where were you last Saturday night when they made that hole across the road over there?'

The day, or rather the night, of the radar-directed Beaufighter was to come later.

The last big daylight raid on London took place on 18th September and marked the end of the first phase of the Blitz. The East End's worst agony was over. By then the night bombing was no longer limited to the docks and the East End and, though this was of course unknown, Hitler had postponed 'Sealion' at least until next spring. The bombing henceforth was to be almost entirely by night and was to be directed against the whole of London, with the admitted purpose of destroying the capital of the British Empire and producing such misery and distress that the populace would compel the Government to sue for peace.

There were two famous incidents during this phase, which have both been very adequately described elsewhere. One was the unexploded bomb that buried itself under St Paul's Cathedral on 12th September, close to the southwest Tower. It was eventually, and after immense trouble, dug out on 15th September by Lieutenant Davies of the Royal Engineers, who was awarded the GC. The details are given by the Dean of St Paul's, Dr Matthews, in his book *St Paul's Cathedral in Wartime*.

The other was the deliberate bombing, in the late morning of the 13th, of Buckingham Palace. King George VI and Queen Elizabeth had a narrow escape, which is graphically described by Sir Winston Churchill in the second volume of his war memoirs. This incident was given considerable publicity, and it undoubtedly heartened the people in the East End to know that their perils were being shared by the highest in the land. In a curious way, this knowledge was

Above right: **King George VI and Queen Elizabeth visit the scene of an 'incident'. The woman they are speaking to survived a direct hit on a shelter which killed twenty people.** *Right:* **Supper-time in an underground shelter**

almost as good for morale as the anti-aircraft barrage.

Before going on to discuss the next phase of the battle, the phase when the shelters were the centre of it all for London's millions, and which lasted until 13th November, a brief summary of the Luftwaffe operations against London during those first twelve days might suitably end this chapter. The night figures, taken from *The Defence of the United Kingdom*, are derived from German archives.

7th September Day
Over 300 bombers bomb the docks and riverside boroughs.
Night
247 bombers drop 335 tons of HE and 440 incendiary canisters, mostly in the dock area.
8th September Day
Little activity
Night
171 bombers drop 207 tons of HE and 327 incendiary canisters, again mostly in the dock area.
9th September Day
Of 200 bombers sent against London, 90 bomb the metropolis.
Night
195 bombers drop 232 tons of HE and 289 incendiary canisters. Target, the docks and the East End.
10th September Day
Little activity.
Night
148 bombers drop 176 tons of HE and 318 incendiary canisters. Target, the docks and the East End.
11th September Day
Heavy attacks on London and Southampton. The RAF lose 29 fighters to 25 enemy planes shot down. The Germans count this a victory.
Night
180 bombers drop 217 tons of HE and 148 incendiary canisters. Partly due to the AA barrage and partly to orders received, there is less concentration on the dock area.

The King and Queen themselves shared the danger, with the bombing of Buckingham Palace

12th September Day
Minor raids.
Night
Only 43 bombers over London, dropping 54 tons of HE and 61 incendiary canisters.
13th September Day
Minor raids.
Night
105 bombers drop 123 tons of HE and 200 incendiary canisters.
14th September Day
Heavy daylight raid on London. 14 RAF fighters destroyed for a similar number of German planes shot down. Göring believes that victory is at hand and Hitler postpones his 'Sealion' decision for three more days.
Night
A light raid on London by 38 bombers dropping 55 tons of HE and 43 incendiary canisters.
15th September Day
More than 200 bombers escorted by some 700 fighters sent against London. 60 enemy planes shot down by the RAF for the loss of 26 fighters. This marked the defeat of the Luftwaffe's attempt to secure air supremacy and thus meant the end of 'Sealion'. This victory is annually celebrated as Battle of Britain day.
Night
181 bombers drop 224 tons of HE and 279 incendiary canisters on London.
16th September Day
Minor raids.
Night
170 bombers drop 189 tons of HE and 318 incendiary canisters on London.
17th September Day
Minor raids. Hitler cancels 'Sealion'.
Night
268 bombers drop 334 tons of HE and 391 incendiary canisters on London.
18th September Day
The last big daylight raid. 70 bombers sent against London, in three waves. 19 shot down by the RAF for the loss of 12 fighters.
Night
The heaviest night raid on London yet. 300 bombers drop 350 tons of HE and 268 incendiary canisters.

Somewhere to sleep

The picture that we have of the Blitz, more perhaps even than that of roaring fires, of collapsing buildings, and of aeroplanes throbbing high in the night sky, is a picture of great communal shelters, of men and women in ungainly attitudes sleeping in huge vaults and under sombre arches, on tube platforms, in the long, thin, pipe-like tunnel of the then uncompleted Liverpool Street extension.

In fact comparatively few people went to such shelters, which were only some of the many forms of shelter available. Though the figures were higher for the public shelters during September and October, by early November – that is to say, while the Blitz in all its intensity was still going on, and when the first shelter census was taken – 60 per cent of the population never went to shelters at all.

Most people who remained in London simply went to bed, at home. They probably modified their arrangements, shifting their beds downstairs, under the stairs if that were possible, when their home was a house. In a block of flats people would move away from the windows, and might have mattresses in the halls or corridors where there was no danger of flying glass. If theirs was the type of house with a basement, they would probably sleep there, having perhaps first reinforced it with beams or double walls and even, occasionally steel struts, often with their most valuable possessions and irreplaceable papers beside them. For most of the middle classes, this was the full extent of the precautions taken. Furthermore, a sort of pride, or even of snobbery, developed about sheltering in public. And there can be little doubt that many people, who would secretly have preferred to go down and down into the deepest of tubes, were held back by the fear of losing

A family settles down for the night in a station on London's underground railway system, the 'tube'

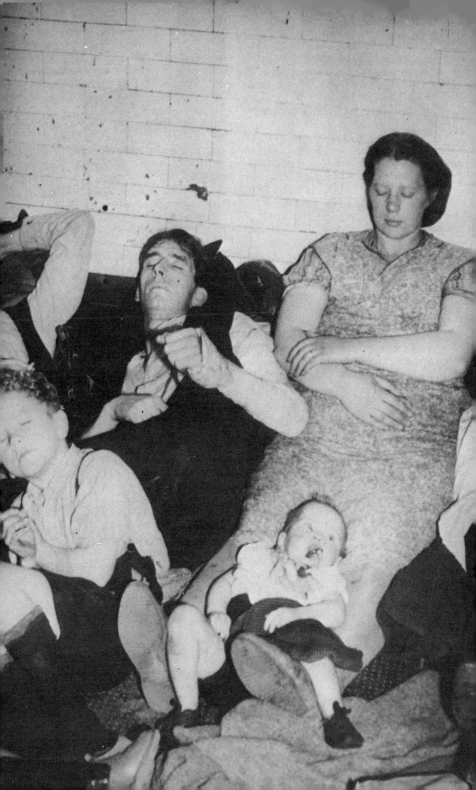

face, for to do so would have meant the admission of another fear; and they had been trained since childhood to believe that the fear of death, though natural enough, is one that must never be displayed.

When houses, as opposed to office blocks, were bombed there were almost always people to be dug out of the rubble, alive or dead, by the rescue services or found in perilous situations on upper floors.

Mr William Sansom tells the story of a Westminster man who arrived home very late, and did not realise that the house in which he lived had been sliced in two. He climbed up the stairs and, luckily for him, went to bed in the half-a-bedroom that still stood. He was brought down by ladder.

There were many very weird escapes. A pretty and extremely respectable Poplar girl was taking a bath when her parents' house was hit. By some fluke, and the effects of bomb blast were often extremely odd, the tub was tipped upside down, with the girl still in it, and thus provided her with shelter from the mass of bricks and rubble in which she was buried. The rescue men dug a shaft from the top to get the buried person out, and when they lifted the tub off her were not unnaturally surprised to discover a beautiful, naked, uninjured girl. Her reaction was one of acute embarrassment: East End girls are very modest. Warden Smith found a flannel night-dress in the rubble, filthy but still better than nothing, and this she gratefully put on at the bottom of the shaft. She was then hoisted up it by means of a block and tackle. Unfortunately on the way up her grimy nightdress caught on a nail or a long splinter, and when she emerged at the top of the ruin she was once again as naked and pink as Venus rising from the Cypriot sea. This time Warden Smith gave her his greatcoat. But so acute was her shame that, as he

rather ruefully remarked, not only did she lack the courage to return him his overcoat, but for years she always crossed to the far side of the Bow Road when she saw him coming towards her.

The most widely used domestic shelter during the Blitz was the Anderson, in which 27 per cent of those who took shelter chose to sleep. (The Morrison, a table-like affair of steel and wire mesh, which was erected in downstairs rooms and which, like the young lady's tub, could support the weight of a small collapsed house, only began to be distributed in the spring of 1941, and therefore played an insignificant part during the big Blitz.) The Anderson fully lived up to expectations. It was never intended to be able to stand up

St Pancras station, devastated by a bomb in October 1940

to a direct hit, but it was able to withstand the blast from a 500lb bomb bursting in the open as near as ten yards away, and on many occasions those small shelters did even better than this.

One of the disadvantages of the Anderson was that, being half buried, and being embanked with earth, it was very liable to fill with water. People did their best to arrange drainage, but this was not simple, and the firemen, in addition to their other very intensive duties, had to spend a lot of time pumping Andersons dry. Nor were they easily warmed in the winter nights. Another disadvantage of the Anderson, as opposed to the communal shelter, was a psychological one. Every crash and roar was audible to the shelterers, and during the raids it soon became apparent that noise was the prime cause of fear. But taken all in all they were extremely successful. Even an Anderson, however, could become a deathtrap.

Hartland Way, by Addington Golf Course in the southern suburbs, is a street of pretty, gardened villas. On 11th September a Royal Air Force fighter crashed into two houses. The petrol from the wreck caught alight and poured, blazing, into a shelter where a young wife with two children and a woman friend had taken cover. They all died.

The brick street shelters, in which 9 per cent of the shelterers slept, were originally intended for passers-by or

A Dornier that ended its mission in Victoria station

for the inhabitants of tenements and flats without the space for the erection of Andersons, and given the inelegant name of 'communal domestic surface shelters'. They enjoyed neither popularity nor a good reputation. This was largely the fault of a Ministry of Home Security clerk and his superiors. Late in 1939, in order to economise on cement, which was in short supply, the Ministry issued an instruction that when building surface shelters lime should replace cement in the ratio of 2:1 in the mortar used. This proved satisfactory. But in April of 1940 the Ministry issued new instructions which were so badly worded that many borough engineers took them to mean that mortar consisting of lime and sand only should now be used. In July the Ministry issued new instructions in which it made plain that ungauged lime mortar must not be used, but no reference was made to the earlier, ambiguous instructions. Thus the brick and concrete shelters built between April and July were left unfortified until the bombs actually fell, whereupon some of them collapsed. The most common disaster was for the roof, a concrete slab, to be lifted by the blast of a nearby bomb and then to crash down again on the brick walls which, being insecurely mortared, would collapse, crushing the shelterers. The solution, which was rapidly carried out, was to build a second, outer wall and also to enlarge the flat concrete roof so that it overlapped the sides and could move a few inches one way or another without falling off its supports.

The brick and concrete shelters, in addition to their unfortunate history, were in some ways the most uncomfortable of all. They lacked the privacy of an Anderson since they held some fifty people, but they did not provide the measure of communal relief to be found in the huge, popular shelters. Also they looked flimsy, and people feared that their flat roofs were conspicuous from the air, and that the German airmen therefore aimed at them deliberately. This was, of course, pure nonsense, but was nonetheless quite widely believed: in some streets the shelterers tried to hide their shelter by covering the flat roof with branches.

The only other type of Government-sponsored shelter, at least in the beginning, was the trench shelter. These were usually in the parks. Many had been dug with almost panic haste during the Munich crisis at the request of the Home Office. To begin with they were simply holes in the ground, but during the following winter the boroughs were told to make these crumbling trenches into permanent shelters, four feet deep, capable of holding 10 per cent of their populations. They were lined and roofed with concrete or steel and were provided with closed entrances, but were not fitted with duckboards, seats or sanitary arrangements. They thus came to resemble narrow surface shelters, half underground and with earth floors. With the outbreak of war in 1939 this programme was accelerated. Large orders were placed for pre-cast concrete trench linings, but these proved unsatisfactory: they not only let in water, but buckled when the raids actually began. These somewhat primitive shelters were supposed to be small, in accordance with the Government's policy of dispersal, and, like the street shelters, to hold about fifty persons each. Many however were considerably larger. Duckboards and benches were installed in some, but not all, of them before the Blitz began. They were more popular than the street shelters; the people felt safer underground and the trench shelters had three feet of earth on top of them. Also they were believed, erroneously, to be warmer. When the Blitz began, they were many people's first choice.

Then there were what the authorities called 'self-chosen' shelters – basements, cellars, arches and other underground places which were, or looked, safe. Some of these had been officially designated as shelters by the boroughs and were strengthened and equipped with blast-proof entrances, anti-gas protection and so on. Others were simply taken over by the people for a number of reasons: because they had been used as shelters in the First World War: because they looked safe: or for quite illogical reasons of mass psychology. Very big buildings, such as railway stations, gave an often quite illusory impression of safety for reasons of size alone: a cellar on a hillside might seem safe, because its entrance was underground, though the greater expanse of the cavern was covered only by one thin roof. These improvised shelters varied enormously, from the utterly safe vaults of huge modern office buildings to the deathtraps that many railway arches proved to be. Some were clean, warm and comfortable, others indescribably filthy and squalid. It usually proved impossible to eject the shelterers from these places, no matter how unsafe and insanitary they might be. The boroughs, and particularly the East End boroughs, thus found themselves in a quandary. Should they do their best to make these unsafe places as safe and as clean as possible? This would seem to justify their continued occupation. On the other hand, could they leave their people in filth and squalor? The answer in most cases seems to have been to leave these improvised shelters uncared for, to begin with, in the hope that the people would move out of them. When they did not do so, and the public outcry became too great, there was a Government enquiry and the outcome was that the boroughs did what they could to improve conditions.

To get the people into the proper shelters, and to discourage them from using the undesirable ones, many expedients were tried. Compulsion was not successful. Persuasion produced

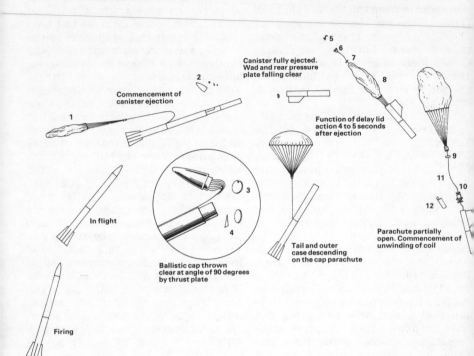

Commencement of canister ejection

Canister fully ejected. Wad and rear pressure plate falling clear

Function of delay lid action 4 to 5 seconds after ejection

1

2

In flight

3

4

Ballistic cap thrown clear at angle of 90 degrees by thrust plate

Firing

Tail and outer case descending on the cap parachute

5

6

7

8

9

11

10

12

Parachute partially open. Commencement of unwinding of coil

PARACHUTE ROCKET
OPERATION AND DEVELOPMENT

One of the major difficulties in using artillery as a means of destroying aircraft is that extreme accuracy is vital and very difficult to attain, and so many powers have considered the idea of explosive charges suspended from parachutes in the flight path of hostile aircraft. The slow rate of sink of the parachute would place the charge in the path of the aircraft longer than would be possible with an ordinary shell. To this end in the last war, the British developed the 3-inch Mark II Shell 'U' Type K. After being fired, the projectile rose above the estimated height of the German bombers and then blew off its ballistic cap at the nose. This released the cap parachute, which in turn braked the tail and casing, ejecting the canister containing the main part of the weapon, a No 7 Bomb Mk IVS.

After this canister had cleared the casing, the rear pressure plate was forced out, and this in turn enabled the main parachute to deploy and pull clear the rest of the weapon, leaving the canister to fall to earth. As the canister fell away, it allowed the 1,000 feet of coiled line to unwind, with the folded towing parachute at the end of it. On striking the wing of an aircraft, the weak link with the main parachute broke, and thereby opened the stabilising parachute, the greater pull of the towing parachute then pulled the bomb onto the wing, where it detonated

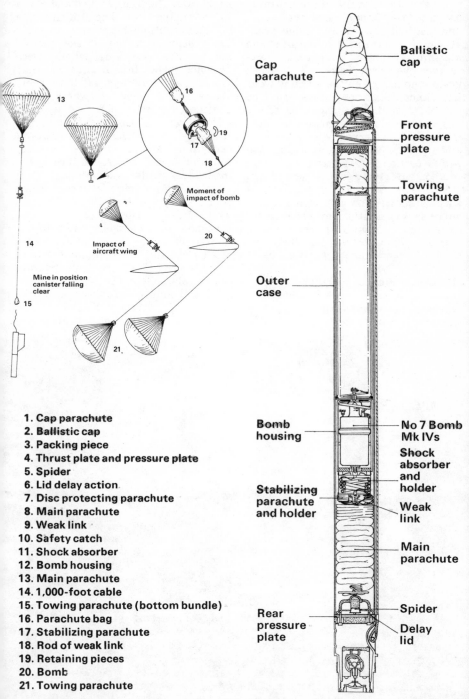

Cap parachute

Ballistic cap

Front pressure plate

Towing parachute

Outer case

Bomb housing

No 7 Bomb Mk IVs

Shock absorber and holder

Stabilizing parachute and holder

Weak link

Main parachute

Rear pressure plate

Spider

Delay lid

13

16

19

17

18

Moment of impact of bomb

14

Impact of aircraft wing

20

15

Mine in position canister falling clear

21

1. Cap parachute
2. Ballistic cap
3. Packing piece
4. Thrust plate and pressure plate
5. Spider
6. Lid delay action
7. Disc protecting parachute
8. Main parachute
9. Weak link
10. Safety catch
11. Shock absorber
12. Bomb housing
13. Main parachute
14. 1,000-foot cable
15. Towing parachute (bottom bundle)
16. Parachute bag
17. Stabilizing parachute
18. Rod of weak link
19. Retaining pieces
20. Bomb
21. Towing parachute

87

better results. In Bethnal Green, in order that the people might be encouraged to use the more suitable shelters, the Council had the clever and original idea of organising open-air dancing in the parks during the fine autumn evenings. The music was relayed over loudspeakers attached to gramophones. When the warning went the dancers and spectators could be easily directed, by loudspeaker, to the proper shelters in or near the park. Order was preserved, chaos avoided and, perhaps equally important, the people tended to arrive at the shelters in a comparatively good humour.

On the other hand, a direct hit on a surface shelter, or a trench shelter, with heavy casualties, would naturally cause much loss of faith in such edifices. In Chelsea, for instance, a reinforced trench shelter in a

The parachute mine, thought by Londoners to be a new weapon, but in fact only an orthodox sea mine wastefully used by Hitler

children's playground, serving a block of working-class flats, was hit in an early raid. The roof cracked and caved in, stunning but not killing five occupants. Simultaneously a water main near that end of the shelter burst. The stunned people were drowned. The inhabitants of that block inevitably lost faith in their shelters and went elsewhere, with considerable bitterness.

It is hardly surprising that in the East End, when the people saw the badly-built street shelters collapse, some preferred to crowd into quite inadequate vaults and cellars.

The most notorious of these great shelters was the Tilbury shelter, which was actually part of the Liverpool Street goods station, off the Commercial Road, Stepney. The story of this shelter is a complicated one, and has a political aspect, in that the Communists led the agitation to occupy it and, when it was occupied, claimed this as a triumph. It was later visited by the Soviet Ambassador,

d the shelterers sang the *Red Flag* thusiastically. The whole business used a lot of head-shaking in hitehall.

The Tilbury shelter, too, had been sed in the First World War. Part of it, llars and vaults, had been taken over a public shelter for 3,000 people the Second World War. The other rt was the loading yard of a huge arehouse, below the level of the ommercial Road, but not of the side ads. Above it the massive warehouse as supported on great steel girders, hich looked safe enough. There were rge loading bays, piled with food and nked by roads and a railroad line. here were outside walls.

Lord Ritchie Calder, who visited the lbury shelter in the early days, has scribed it in these words:

'When the official shelter was owded out, those in charge of the her parts allowed the people to use , on compassionate grounds. The sult was unbelievable. Estimates the numbers using this expropriated elter varied, but on a wet night hen I was there, extra people came in om their domestic shelter which d flooded, and the shelter wardens lculated that in the two halves there ere over 14,000 people.

'People queued up from midday, aiting for the gates to open at four-irty in the afternoon. Service men leave kept places for their families t at work. Unevacuated school-ildren were "proxies" for their latives. Old folks in bathchairs, ipples, children in perambulators, d men and women of every age and ndition lined up, oblivious of day-ght sirens and even dog-fights over-ad, because if they took shelter they st their places in the queue and their ption" on their favourite sleeping-ot for the night. When the gates ere opened the police linked hands stem the rush down the slope, but it as like holding back a stampede of ffaloes. Usually a way was made r the aged, and for mothers with rambulators and young children

(although the police got wise to the fact that they were getting priority for perambulators which contained not babies, but the family valuables). Sometimes women and children got crushed in the rush.

'At night, it presented a scene unequalled by anything west of Suez. One had to pick one's way along the roads between the recumbent bodies. Until the Ministry of Food intervened and had the cartons of margarine and the other food stuffs removed, people slept in the bays, beside or on the food. To begin with there was practically no sanitary provision, and the filth seeped into the blankets or was spread by trampling feet. Cartons filled with margarine were sometimes stacked up to form latrines.

'Every race and colour in the world were represented there – Whites, Negroes, Chinese, Hindus, Polyne-sians, Levantines, East Europeans, Jews, Gentiles, Moslems, and probably Sun-Worshippers were all piled there in miscellaneous confusion. Seamen came in for a few hours between tides. Prostitutes paraded. Hawkers sold clammy fried fish, which cloyed the fug with greasy sickliness. The police broke up free fights. And children slept.'

Strange as it may seem, some people from the West End used to go sight-seeing to this and other such shelters, even as before the war they would make up jolly parties to visit Chinatown or do a riverside pub-crawl in Wapping. Needless to say, slumming of this sort was not at all popular with the shelterers singing their songs of solidarity in Stepney, and at least one party of sight-seers was quite roughly handled before being ejected. But for those whose tastes ran to such spectacles, there was plenty to be seen, and smelt, in the tubes for the trifling cost of a ticket.

The Government's policy of keeping the tubes free of shelterers failed almost at once. The people simply bought a 1½d. ticket, went down below, and remained there. To turn

them out into the raids would have needed not only a huge police force but also a callousness which was not greatly in evidence at this time.

The number of people using the tubes for shelter reached its maximum in late September – according to the London Passenger Transport Board's publication *London Transport Carried On*, on 27th September, with 177,000 people in the tubes – and then gradually declined. During the raids in the winter and spring the number averaged something over 100,000, on raid-free nights between 70,000 and 80,000.

In the beginning it was all confusion. In the early days shelterers were allowed into the tubes after four o'clock in the afternoon, but not before. Therefore, to be sure of obtaining a place, women would start to queue outside the tube stations, or would send their children to queue for them, as early as ten o'clock in the morning. The gangs of youths who used to make a spivish living selling places in theatre queues, now turned to these more vital queues since there were no theatres open. They would do queuing, would dump bundles of rags to mark a 'reserved' place on the platform, and would sell these places for varying sums, half a crown being considered an excessive but not exorbitant charge. The transport officials and the police, meanwhile, did their best to keep at least part of the platforms clear for travellers by painting two white lines, one eight feet and the other four feet from the platform's outer edge. Until half past seven, the shelterers were not supposed to cross the eight-foot line. After the rush hours, and until half past ten, four feet of platform were kept clear for travellers. At half past ten the train service was discontinued, the lights dimmed (at the request of the shelterers) but not extinguished,

One of the tube stations converted into a shelter by filling in the area where the line once ran

the current cut off in the electric rail. The shelterers, who had hitherto in some cases passed a social evening with cards, sing-songs, and banter, now had the whole station to themselves, and usually settled down to sleep all over the platforms, in the passages, on the escalators, some actually between the rails. They were turned out very early next morning.

That staying in the tubes was uncomfortable is certain. Among the minor inconveniences were a plague of mosquitoes which haunted the tubes that winter, refusing to hibernate owing to the warmth engendered by all those packed bodies: the winds which howl, now hot now cold, through the tunnels (later the shelterers requested that the ventilator fans be turned off after ten thirty, and in many stations this was done: the lice which caused the medical authorities considerable anxiety: the stench of human excrement from the tunnels, before lavatories were installed: and, of course, the hardness of the stone platforms, and the crowding. No matter. The tubes were believed to be, and in many cases were, safe, but only the deepest ones. This the people failed to realise. The result was that they crowded into tube stations which were later hit, with numerous casualties. On successive October nights, Trafalgar Square Station was hit (seven killed), Bounds Green (nineteen killed, all but three of them Belgian refugees who occupied one end of the platform, a pathetic colony), Praed Street (eight killed) and, worst of all, on 14th October, Balham.

The Balham tube station roof is some thirty feet below Balham High Road, and between the road and the tube is the usual intricate tangle of water mains, sewer mains, electric light and telephone cables and gas conduits. These were smashed. Water from the mains and sewers ran into the tube station, where about 600 people were sheltering, first a trickle, then a torrent, finally a river three feet deep bringing with it tons of sand

Breakfast in the street, the morning after the bombing

and rubble. There was a stench of commercial gas. A motorman, employed by the LPTB, has described what he saw in these words:

'It was about 8 pm. I was standing on the platform talking to people when there was this terrific explosion above the station and at the same time one of the platform lamps "arced", and that put the station in darkness. When the station went into darkness panic started; it was bad panic. I said to them: "It will be all right; we will have a light on in a few minutes."

'There were a lot of women and children, including my own wife and two children, and I was talking to them. When I was saying we could soon get a light, I didn't realise that the tunnel had collapsed. Then there was a smell of gas, and the children were shouting out for their gas-masks. I got my torch and flashed it up and saw water was pouring down in torrents.

'I thought it was time something was done to get these people out. I went back and opened the emergency hatch. I got the people more dis-ciplined and they filed through the escape hatch in single file. It took some ten minutes to pass them through the hatch – about seventy or eighty of them. I told them to come up the escalator, to wait in the booking hall, and the rescue squad came along and took my torch and I had to manage without one.

'All this time water was pouring in and I was up to my knees in water. Soon it was like a waterfall. In about five minutes all the anti-suicide pits were full. The water went up to about the second stair of the escalator.'

Seven years later, according to Mr Charles Graves, this motorman still had scars on his hands caused by people tearing at them while he was trying to draw the bolts of the emergency hatch.

The attitude of the Government, and hence of the boroughs, to the whole shelter problem underwent two major changes during the first few weeks of the Blitz.

The policy of dispersal had proved a partial failure so far as central London and the East End were concerned. The big, commandeered shelters and tubes existed. If the people were not to be

ejected – and this was not a course that was seriously advocated – something must be done to minimise the dangers which had led the Government to oppose mass sheltering from the beginning. There were three main dangers: that to physical health, in the form of epidemics: that to mental health, in the form of progressive demoralisation, hysteria, absenteeism and all that was contained in the phrase 'deep-shelter mentality': and, closely connected with the latter, that of large incidents involving heavy and shocking casualties.

As early as 14th September, that is to say just one week after the heavy bombing started, the Minister of Health and the Minister of Home Security appointed a committee, under the chairmanship of Lord Horder, whose frame of reference was to enquire into 'the conditions of air raid shelters used for sleeping purposes, with particular reference to health'. The Horder Committee, working with what must be almost record speed for such enquiries, made their initial recommendations four days later.

The Horder Committee regarded overcrowding in the 'self-chosen' shelters as the main danger. It therefore advocated an intensive publicity campaign to persuade the people to remain in their Andersons and their communal surface shelters, and also advocated that these should be made more attractive: the Andersons should be provided with bunks, entrance curtains and light: the communal surface shelters should be assigned to specified residents 'who should be entitled to regard them as their own (and who, if there are doors, should be provided with keys)'. These suggestions, which were carried out to a certain extent in some of the boroughs, do not seem to have persuaded many people to leave their 'self-chosen' shelters. As already pointed out, the motives that had led them to the arches and cellars were emotional, not logical. On the other hand, they probably helped to prevent more people from abandoning their Andersons and street shelters.

The Horder Committee suggested that the boroughs examine all the 'self-chosen' shelters and attempt to find more of similar type to relieve congestion. The boroughs should then approve such shelters which reached a decent standard of protection and hygiene. This was done, and gradually took effect.

It was proposed that the boroughs pool their shelter resources, a purely administrative matter, that the factory shelters not in use at night be opened to the public, and that 'the possibility of using the tube system for shelters during the night be considered'. This last suggestion was already long out of date: the problems in the tubes were almost the same by then as the problems of the other 'self-chosen' shelters, that is to say, crowding and an absence of hygiene.

The aged, the infirm, the bedridden and as many young children as possible should be evacuated. By early November 4,000 of the former had been moved from London shelters to hospitals in the country and more were going. Tens of thousands of children went, some with and some without their mothers.

The four final recommendations were all of a more positive nature, and were also carried out. Shelter marshals were appointed. The local authorities were told to install sanitary equipment. The Medical Officer of Health was to make regular inspection of the shelters, and First Aid Points were to be provided.

The question of ventilation and heating was gone into, and to reduce the dangers of infections, shelters should be, and were, sprayed regularly with a cheap antiseptic, sodium hypochlorite in aqueous solution.

Such, then, were the basic medical recommendations. They produced results which astonished the doctors. There was no influenza epidemic, no diphtheria epidemic, no great increase in respiratory diseases such as tuberculosis. In fact the health of the shelterers does not appear to have suffered at all during the months spent in the stuffy, crowded arches and tubes. Indeed the provision of First Aid Posts, each with a trained nurse and many with a doctor as well, enabled the shelterers to have immediate medical attention for maladies and indispositions which in many cases would otherwise have gone unchecked. Within a few weeks, too, the necessary sanitary arrangements were installed.

The morale factor in the shelters was in some ways more difficult, in others easier, to tackle. The first problem was to provide a modicum of comfort. Heat and light were laid on quite rapidly. But towards the end of the year as installation of wire bunks began, a surprising amount of opposition was met from the shelterers themselves. These bunks, three-tiered wooden frames (later replaced by metal frames, since the wood harboured lice), of which the centre one could be raised so as to make them into seats when not in use as beds, occupied considerable space. A shelter, or a tube platform, equipped with bunks could not hold as many shelterers as one without. This meant that in the crowded shelters a number of people would have to go elsewhere. A ticket to a bunk was allotted to each shelterer. The result on occasion was anger, amounting to rebellion.

In some East End shelters the shelterers, having become accustomed to sleeping on the floor, quite refused to use the bunks.

The atmosphere in the shelters varied of course greatly from district to district, and even from shelter to shelter. Thus in Bethnal Green one former shelter marshal, a woman, tells this story:

'I used to try hard to get the children into their bunks for their night's rest, but it was very difficult, because all the crowds of adults sitting there talking and laughing would keep the children awake. So I hit on a scheme to have a penny raffle a week off of every one of the people that was in the shelter, which they quite agreed to do. And with these pennies I used to go and buy all the cheap little sweets that I could get. And I used to say to the kiddies: "Now, come on, the first one of you which is undressed and in bed gets a nice sweet!" And there used to be such a scramble for them all to get into their bunks to see who would be the first one to get their sweet! And perhaps this sweet was only just a little tiny toffee, or a liquorice allsort, or something like that, but they used to be thrilled, and they'd get into their bunks, cover themselves up, have their sweet and go to sleep.'

Another Post Warden, a very small woman also in Bethnal Green, has said:

'In one of my shelters unbeknown to us they moved in a piano, and of course the first I heard of it was that they'd all come out of the pub and it was a proper bedlam. They said it was like Barley Fair over there. They was

The eternally popular pastime, played late into the night in the crowded shelters

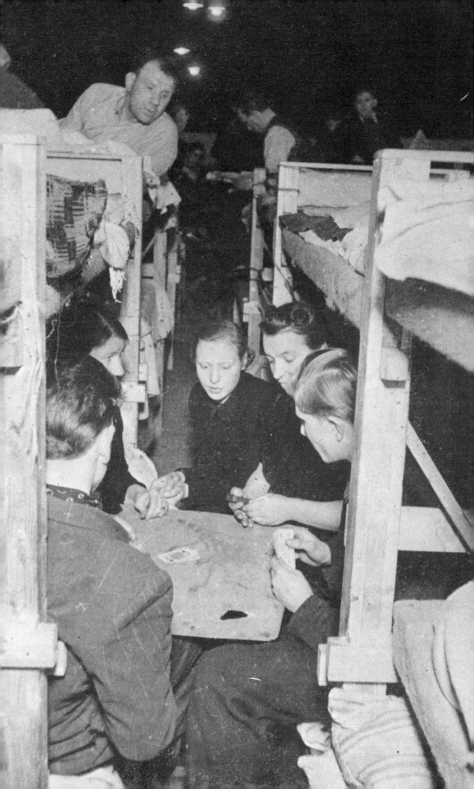

singing and dancing, and they said: "You'd better come over, Doll, because you know the people and you can deal with 'em." Well, I will say this. I grew up with some of these people, and rough as they was, they didn't make it too hard. But I had a nasty one among them now and then. I could handle them. But my shelter wardens, they couldn't do nothing with them. They moved the piano once, and it came in again. Finally it got so bad we had to get the Town Hall to do something about it. Because people did want their rest, and up to a certain time, yes, you're allowed a singsong, like you was in an ordinary house, but when you went into the early morning it had to be stopped – and let other people get their rest . . . Because if you got a bad night in the shelter you didn't feel as if you could work next day. Oh, I might tell you we had some lively times, mouthorgans in one, the piano in the other. . .'

In yet a third Bethnal Green shelter, the shelter warden, a man, has said:

'The only entertainment we had was the Church used to come in there and hold a service, but then that had to stop because the kiddies used to come in there eating potatoes and hot dogs, running around, some fetching their homework in, making stools for the shelter, so that fell off.' This seems to have been an argumentative shelter. 'Yes, there was Belgian Jews, Russian Jews, all nationalities, and my job, well, I couldn't understand a word they was saying. And there'd be a little argument going on, I used to go round and ask if there was anyone who could speak their language. By the time I got back to them there'd be another little argument started a little way along, then I'd start all over again.'

But still, the bunks were installed and the tickets issued – in the tubes, for sleeping space on the platforms as well as for the bunks – and thus by the end of the year, or at least early in

The familiar queue as Londoners wait for their shelter to open

1941, a certain order was established. People had their homes above ground, with their Anderson shelter to sleep in, or they had a bed, their semi-permanent property, down below ground. And in this underground half-world, there were gradually installed some of the amenities of war-time civilisation, with canteens, medical attention, even entertainment and culture of a sort. In Bermondsey, amateur actors toured the shelters, with a production of Chekhov's *The Bear*, while the shelterers in the Swiss Cottage tube station produced their own magazine entitled *The Swiss Cottager*. In some boroughs the indefatigable and admirable ladies of the WVS organised sewing bees and lectures. South of the river the soldiers of 167 Coy, Pioneer Corps, engaged on clearing rubble, soon had a concert party going, which performed in the shelters six nights a week for thirteen weeks. And here we are moving away from the purely indigenous relaxation, of which the pack of cards and the Bethnal Green mouthorgans are perhaps the archetypes, into more sophisticated forms of entertainment, sent down to the shelterers from above.

Library services were organised, 4,000 paperback books being provided for the West Ham shelterers alone. Not everywhere were religious services made impossible by hot-dog-eating children, and in Bermondsey we learn that they were appreciated by many, though care was taken not to offend or irritate the irreligious, for a contemporary document says: 'Wherever possible the services are conducted in places where only those who wish for a service need come.' The large shelters had film shows, and the authorities took advantage of this most popular entertainment to insert a short public health film in each programme. By January of 1941 the London County Council were holding more than 200 classes in the shelters, on such subjects as current affairs and dress-making. PT classes were planned

for the boys and girls. Anarchy, in fact, was well under control. Dartboards were supplied, and darts leagues organised, shelter *v* shelter. The Council for the Encouragement of Music and the Arts (the fore-runner of the Arts Council) sent people into the shelters with gramophones and albums of classical music. It was the job of the person who worked the gramophone, we are told, to 'explain the meaning of the music and the circumstances in which it was written'.

This amelioration of the conditions of the tubes and large shelters was in itself a change of Government policy, dictated by the nature of the raids. Throughout October there was a raid on London every night: only on two nights did less than sixty planes bomb the metropolis: and usually these raids lasted from dusk till dawn. These were conditions very different from those envisaged before the war, when the shelter policy was laid down against the expectation of short, sharp raids killing many thousands of people. Instead there was this steady, all-night pulverisation of London's buildings, with far fewer casualties than had been expected. (In October almost 5,000 tons of high explosive were dropped on London, causing fatal casualties at the approximate rate of one per ton dropped, while only 6,343 people were detained in hospital. When it is realised that at no time were there less than 120,000 beds available in London hospitals for air raid casualties, it is seen again how enormously the fear had surpassed the reality.)

On the other hand, there seemed then no reason why this steady pounding away at London should not continue indefinitely, for months and perhaps for years. Sir Winston Churchill has written: 'Our outlook at this time (October) was that London, except for its strong modern buildings, would be gradually and soon reduced to a rubble-heap.' The RAF and AA Command were still shooting down almost no enemy night bombers, and though great, and justified, hopes were placed in the radar equipment which was about to be issued both to the night fighters and to the guns, it was always possible that the Germans would find an answer to this defensive weapon.

Indeed it was expected that the bombing would get worse. When the Blitz started the Germans had few big bombs. In 1940, 99 per cent of the bombs dropped weighed 250 kilograms or less, the 250-kilo and the 50-kilo high explosive bomb being the standard models. It was against bombs of this size that the pre-war shelter programme had been designed. But heavier bombs were on the way. The RAF were thinking of making larger bombs, and it was assumed, quite correctly, that the Germans were doing likewise. Indeed, a few 1,000-kilo and a very occasional 2,500-kilo bomb were being dropped, as well as quite large numbers of mines attached to parachutes. In general a 1,000-kilo bomb does far more damage than four of 250-kilo each, and a 2,500-kilo bomb is worth much more than fifty weighing 50-kilo, provided the engineering problem of making all the high explosive explode simultaneously is overcome. It was clear that the Germans realised this, since one reason for their dropping expensive 500- or 1,000-kilo sea mines against land targets was their shortage of heavy bombs (as these mines exploded on impact, without burying themselves, the radius of blast was very great: on the other hand, being ill-fused for use against land targets, some 20 per cent of the 4,000 dropped failed to explode.) In fact all the evidence pointed towards an indefinitely continued bombardment of London, but with heavier bombs than those now used. And as Sir Winston has said: 'If the bombs of 1943 had been applied to the London of 1940, we should have passed into conditions that might have pulverised all human organisation.'

Certainly, apart from the deep tubes, there were then no shelters available to withstand the heavier bombs that must be expected. In October, therefore, the whole deep-shelter policy was reversed. It was decided to begin work immediately on the construction of eight deep-level shelters, branching like the spokes of eight wheels from existing deep tube stations, to hold 64,000 shelterers. These, together with the deep tubes, would hold rather more shelterers than the present number sleeping in large, public shelters. This work was put in hand, at vast expense, but none of these deep shelters was ready by the time the Blitz was over. Later in the war some of them were used as shelters or as headquarters and billets for troops.

Meanwhile little could be done to make the existing shelters any safer, though wherever possible this was attempted. For the rest, it was an endless job of repairs, repairs to the public utilities first of all, and repairs to houses. Every night saw gas mains cut, water mains destroyed, railway lines blasted, roads cratered. Every morning what repairs were possible were made. In Poplar, by the end of the year, the total of houses damaged exceeded the total number of houses: many had been damaged more than once. Nor was Poplar unique in this distinction. In October the main sewage outfall was destroyed, and raw sewage was pouring into the Thames which stank, in Sir Winston's phrase, 'first of sewage and afterwards of the floods of chemicals we poured into it'. The vast intricacy of cables and pipes posed endless problems to the gas, water and light repair squads. A broken water main in Bruton Street was found to be made of curiously shaped wooden pipes, laid down in ancient times. A carpenter had to make replacements. The cemeteries were hit, and the dead of bygone centuries tossed up into the battered streets.

That was London, in October of 1940, when there seemed no reason why the bombing should not go on for years.

Strange things from the sky

In an Order of the Day issued to his air crews on 18th October, Göring, the Commander-in-Chief of the Luftwaffe, said: 'Your indefatigable, courageous attacks on the head of the British Empire, the City of London with its eight and a half million inhabitants, have reduced the British plutocracy to fear and terror.' And for the next month his air crews continued dutifully to drop most of their bombs on the plutocrats' capital. The first raid-free night that London had known since 7th September was that of 3rd–4th November, but on the next night the bombers were back, and for a further ten days there were once again heavy raids each night. On 14th November Coventry was the target, but on the 15th, 16th and 17th it was once again London. And then German strategy changed.

Just as the target had been expanded from the East End to London as a whole in late September so, in late November, it was again expanded from London to almost all the major industrial cities of the United Kingdom. From mid-November until late January the Luftwaffe was over Britain in great strength almost every night on which flying was at all possible, but from 18th November to 19th January, out of twenty-eight raids by one hundred or more planes, only six were directed against London, while out of eleven light raids London was the target for two, both of which were diversions while the main weight of the Luftwaffe attacked provincial cities.

From 19th January to 8th March there was a lull. This period saw only five comparatively light raids: one on London on 29th January, two on Swansea in February, and two on Cardiff in early March.

Heavy bombing began again on 8th March, when 120 bombers were over London, and continued almost with-

Coventry Cathedral, destroyed when the Luftwaffe changed its strategy to attack industrial targets

Another provincial city that suffered. Volunteer workers provide soup and sandwiches for the people made homeless in Liverpool

The damage in Coventry

out interruption until mid-May, but now London was once again only one target among many. It suffered two more heavy, and one very heavy, raids in March: two very heavy raids in April, known to Londoners as 'the Wednesday' and 'the Saturday', both of which were specifically ordered by Hitler as reprisals for the bombing of Berlin: and one very heavy raid in May.

The reason for this change of strategy is not hard to see. Though the plutocrats of West Ham, Balham and Battersea had been quite badly knocked about by the bombs of the National Socialists, their top hats dented and their morning coats hideously begrimed, they showed not the slightest sign, visible across the Channel, of any wish to surrender. In fact the attempt to force the British to capitulate by bombing the concentration of civilians living and working within fifteen miles of Charing Cross

had apparently failed. The Germans, therefore, decided to try the third of their plans for conquering Britain: 'Attack on the English air arm and on the country's war economy and its resources as a whole'. This new policy was inaugurated with the very heavy and destructive raid on Coventry, where so many factories vital to the aircraft industry and war production generally were located, on 14th November. Henceforth, with the exception of Hitler's two reprisal raids in April, London was attacked as an industrial centre rather than as a centre of population (though this subtle distinction was scarcely perceptible to the people whose families were killed or houses destroyed in these later raids).

If there were doubts, even at an early stage, in the German High Command concerning the efficacy of the attacks on London's morale, and if these resulted in a certain vacillation and a perhaps premature change of strategy, tactically the air attacks were carried out with maximum intensity and in maximum strength. A German air force staff officer has stated that even after mid-November, when heavy attacks were being directed against the ports and the industrial cities, London remained the principal target.

Had the active defences been stronger, it would have been necessary for the Germans to attempt to swamp them by concentrating all their bombers over the target at one time. As it was, concentration of attack was not necessary in the early months, and hardly more so later, though the gunners were becoming more successful (the number of shells fired per aircraft shot down, which had been 30,000 in September, dropped to 11,000 in October, to about 7,000 in November and December, and to 4,000 in January, by which time there were a considerable number of radar-directed guns in action). They did not claim many kills at night: 22 in October, 21 in November and only 14 in December. A former German bomber pilot has said that the sight of the A A barrage, with shells bursting at all heights, did on occasion worry inexperienced crews, but he adds that since so few planes were shot down they soon became accustomed to these fireworks. The night-fighters did not begin to show success on any significant scale until March. Thus in 1940 the Germans could bomb London by night almost as and when they chose.

The bomber units came in on separate courses and at different heights, usually between 9,000 feet (which put them above the range of the light and medium anti-aircraft guns), and 12,000 feet. On occasions there were as many as three different 'layers' of bombers over London simultaneously. But normal tactics were to space out the attacks. To increase the strain on civilian morale, the duration of the raids was deliberately prolonged to the maximum, and raids lasting ten, twelve, even fourteen hours were not unusual. In the more massive raids, bomber crews would make two sorties over London in one night, and during the two great reprisal raids of April, 1941, some crews even made three, a veritable shuttle service between their bases beyond the Channel and the target area.

On moonlit nights attempts were made to bomb specific targets in London. In the beginning units – wings or groups – were allotted particular targets. On moonless nights the whole conurbation was bombed, though even so an attempt was usually made to establish some sort of bomb-dropping zone by sending over a pathfinder group ahead of the main bomber force. This force was the celebrated Kampfgeschwader 100, 'the Fireraisers'. Originally only a wing, but later expanded to a group, this unit had various electronic aids to navigation to help it pin-point the target. The two best-known of these were the so-called X-apparatus and the Y-apparatus. The former consisted, roughly, of two radio beams between which the bomber flew. These beams were laid to intersect above the target. On reaching the point of intersection, the bombardier simply released his bombs, while some planes were even equipped with an automatic bomb release mechanism geared to the beam reception. The Y-apparatus was a single beam which sent back an echo from the bomber to the station whence it emanated. It was thus possible for the ground control to calculate how far the bomber had travelled along the beam, and when it was over the target to order the release of the bomb-load.

An intensive, secret struggle took place between the British and the German scientists. The British put out false beams parallel to those of the X-apparatus, to lure the German bombers off course: they also 'bent' the Y-beam. Some British night fighters were equipped with apparatus for picking up the beam and thus, it was hoped, would be in a position to

Anti-aircraft gun overlooking the English Channel

intercept the incoming bombers. This struggle, however, was at a discount so far as London is concerned. The city presented so huge a target, and one so close to the German bases, that navigational aids were a luxury rather than a necessity.

Nevertheless the beams were used in the bombing of London. They were not usually very accurate. For example, on the night that the City burned, 29th December 1940, the bombers were led in by the He111s of KG100 flying on X-beams. The map prepared for the night's operation shows that the beams were intended to intersect roughly over Piccadilly Circus. In fact KG 100 unloaded its marker bombs some two miles further to the east, in the neighbourhood of St Paul's Cathedral.

During the early winter, a German air force staff officer has said, the Luftwaffe kept up its attacks almost regardless of the weather, often flying in conditions which, in the past, would have been deemed very dangerous or even impossible. When the Ju 88s and the He 111s could not operate because they needed a longer runway for take-off and had a higher landing speed, the more antiquated Do 17s flew alone. As a result of these tactics the losses due to bad weather conditions (such as faulty landing, icing up and baling out when badly off course) well outnumbered the losses inflicted by the British defences. The operational strength of the Luftwaffe's bombers in the West began to decline, from approximately 860 on 1st September, to 820 on 1st October and to only a little over 700 on 1st December. And the number of bombers over the target declined accordingly. During the last twelve raids of September the average number was 197: during the last twelve of October 134: and during the first twelve of November 128. Still, the Germans went on for several more weeks putting everything they could into the air. And by making great efforts, involving double sorties, they still managed to mount an occasional 300- or even 400-bomber raid in December. But this tempo could not be maintained into the new year. A telling factor was the rapid deterioration, in wet weather, of the bomber fields in France and the Low Countries, only a few of which had runways and concrete taxi-ing lanes. During the January raids the number of bombers over the target averaged only 120, and from late January until early March bombing operations against Britain were almost discontinued.

An important contributory cause

so this lull in the bombing was dictated by German strategy on the highest level. In December of 1940 the decision was taken to invade Russia early in the following summer. Hitler could not afford to let his bomber force be wasted away in accidents. And the lull gave the German Air Force a chance to rebuild its bomber strength and to bring its operational units up to full establishment. This was done. When the Blitz was renewed in March, the German bomber force in the West – despite transfers to the Italo-African and Balkan theatres of war – was as strong numerically as it had been in September. It had also been partially re-equipped with new types of planes, or improved models of the older ones, and heavier bombs were now available.

The German attack on London would have been much more cruel in 1940 had they not had to rely chiefly on comparatively light bombs. They were well aware of this, and one expedient that they used was to drop sea-mines by parachute against land targets.

The magnetic mines had been Hitler's first 'secret weapon' of the war, and had caused very heavy losses of shipping during the winter of 1939–40. It had been largely mastered, through the degaussing of ships and other means, by the summer of 1940, though it was still a menace. The original method of delivery had been for surface vessels to sow their mines in British coastal waters, but in November of 1939 seaplanes began to drop them by parachute. Later landplanes were also used for this purpose, the Heinkel 111s of Kampfgeschwader 4 being equipped each to carry two magnetic mines, slung beneath their wings on either side of the fuselage. By the time the Blitz began these magnetic mines, as weapons in the sea war, were becoming obsolescent, and since the Germans lacked a big blast bomb, they immediately began to use them against land targets. On the very first day of the Blitz, KG 4 and other bomber groups were dropping mines on parachutes into the dock area; according to a pilot of that group, he and his comrades were thenceforth usually taken off their normal mine-laying duties whenever there was a major raid on London and were sent out as an ordinary bomber group, sometimes with bombs, sometimes with mines. In the beginning, these were dropped complete with sea-fuse, though later the sea-fuses were removed. This expenditure of mines against land targets did not altogether please the German Navy.

On 20th September Raeder told Hitler: 'At present numerous aerial mines are being dropped on London. . . They have a decided effect, to be sure; however, the time has come for large-scale mine operations, since the new type of fuse is now available in sufficient quantities.' This is a reference to the acoustic fuse. The Luftwaffe, wishing to use the mines as bombs, pulled the other way, and by 14th October Hitler had authorised a compromise whereby the Air Force was allowed to drop the 'old sort of mines' over London on moonlit nights, when, presumably, these expensive objects could, in theory at least, be aimed at targets of commensurate value. And throughout the Blitz these great cylinders, weighing a ton or a ton and a half each, came silently swinging down through the night skies on to the streets and houses of the capital.

It is a curious coincidence that whereas Hitler ordered that they be dropped on moonlit nights in order that some accuracy be obtained, Churchill, four weeks earlier, on 19th September had written in a memorandum for the Chiefs of Staff Committee: 'The dropping of large mines by parachute proclaims the enemy's enitre abandonment of all pretence of aiming at military objectives. At 5,000 feet he cannot have the slighest idea of what he is going to hit. This, therefore, proves the "act of terror" intention against the civil popula-

The Dornier Do 17Z was a greatly improved variant of the original Do 17 design, incorporating the lessons learnt in the Spanish Civil War. Functional design, the need to incorporate armament to defend the belly of the aircraft, overcame aerodynamic efficiency. In common with other Luftwaffe bombers, the crew was all grouped in the nose compartment. Designed as a tactical weapon, the Do 17 was out of its depth when trying to fulfil a strategic role such as the bombing of London. With anything but a full load of bombs its offensive power was severely curtailed, but with a full load range was extremely critical. *Crew :* 4. *Engines :* Two Bramo Fafnir 323 radials, 1,000 hp each at take off. *Armament :* 2,200 pounds of bombs and six 7.9mm machine-guns. *Speed :* 255mph at 13,120 feet. *Range :* 720 miles *Ceiling :* 27,000 feet. *Weight empty/loaded :* 11,484/19,481 pounds. *Span :* 59 feet 0⅓ inch. *Length :* 51 feet 9⅔ inches

tion.' Certainly these mines, called almost universally and quite incorrectly 'land mines', did inspire great terror. This was due primarily to the violence of the explosion, no part of which was muffled (as with the occasional bombs of similar weight then being dropped) by burial in the ground; but a secondary cause was the usual spooky silence with which those lethal monsters came floating down. For instance one that dropped, silently, on to the Park Hill recreation grounds in Croydon, on 28th September, broke all the windows in the High Street, a good ten minutes' walk away.

And here is a description of another, which fell outside the BBC, in Langham Place, and destroyed, among other building, the old Langham Hotel. It is a transcript of a recording made for the BBC during the war. The narrator is a man, and few people who were so close to a mine when it exploded can have survived to tell the tale:

'On the night of 8th December 1940, I left the BBC shortly after ten forty-five and accompanied by a colleague, Mr Sibbick, went to the cycle-shed in Chapel Mews. The customary nightly air-raid was in progress, and as we left the cycle-shed we could hear the distant sound of aircraft and AA gun-fire. We were just entering Hallam Street from the mews when I heard the shrieking whistling noise like a large bomb falling. This noise continued for about three seconds, and then abruptly ceased as if in mid-air. There was no thud, explosion or vibration. I particularly remember this, as I'd heard this happen once before, and was curious as to what caused it and why it stopped. Then came the sound of something clattering down the roof of a building in the direction of Broadcasting House. looked up thinking that it might be incendiaries, but this was not so. We slowly walked round to the entrance of Broadcasting House, and I estimate that we took about three and a half minutes in doing so. My colleague went inside, returned the cycle-shed keys, cycled off towards Oxford Circus I remained outside the entrance talking to two policemen, and enquiring about possible diversions on my route home. Their names were Vaughan and Clarke. A saloon car was parked alongside the curb some distance round from the entrance, and

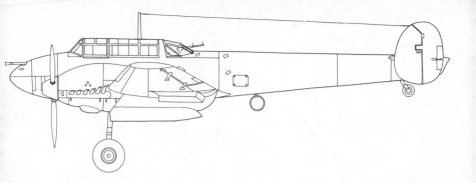

The Messerschmitt Bf 110 was designed as a long range fighter, but it proved vulnerable in that role to more nimble Allied types. It was then developed into a useful escort and night fighter, in which role it proved more successful. Specification for Bf 110C. *Crew:* 2. *Engines:* Two Daimler-Benz DB 601A inlines, 1,100hp each. *Armament:* five 7.9mm machine guns and two 20mm cannon. *Speed:* 349mph at 23,000 feet. *Range:* 500 miles. *Ceiling:* 32,000 feet. *Weight loaded:* 15,300 pounds. *Span:* 53 feet $4\frac{7}{8}$ inches. *Length:* 39 feet $8\frac{1}{2}$ inches

I could see to the left of the car the lamp-post in the middle of the road opposite the Langham Hotel. The policemen had their backs to this, so did not observe what followed. Whilst we were conversing I noticed a large, dark, shiny object approach the lamp-post and then recede. I concluded that it was a taxi parking. It made no noise. The night was clear, with a few small clouds. There was moonlight from a westerly direction, but Portland Place was mainly shadow. All three of us were wearing our steel helmets; my chinstrap was round the back of my head, as I had been advised to wear it so shortly after I was issued with the helmet.

'A few seconds later I saw what seemed to be a very large tarpaulin of a drab or khaki colour fall on the same spot; the highest part of it was about ten or twelve feet above the road when I first saw it, and it seemed to be about twenty-five feet across. It fell at about the speed of a pocket handkerchief when dropped, and made no noise. Repair work was being carried out on Broadcasting House and I, not unnaturally, concluded that it was a tarpaulin which had become detached

and had fallen from the building into the roadway. There were no other warnings of any imminent danger. I drew the attention of the policemen to it. They turned round and could see nothing. It had collapsed, and from where we were it was partly screened by the car, and the roadway at that point was in shadow. They told me that they could not see anything. Then followed some banter, but I persisted in saying that I had seen something fall in the road. They then decided to go to investigate. A third policeman, Mortimer, had meanwhile approached us – he was about to conduct a lady across that part of the road. But after hearing that I'd seen something he told me that he was taking her inside the building while they found out what it was. Vaughan drew ahead of Clarke, who stopped at the curb to ask me just exactly where it had dropped. I went over towards him, calling out that I would show him it. It was about a minute since I'd seen the dark object. I went towards the tarpaulin and had reached a spot to the left of Clarke about six feet from the curb, and twenty-five to thirty feet from "the thing", when Vaughan came

running towards me at high speed. He shouted something which I did not hear. At that moment there was a very loud swishing noise, as if a plane were diving with engine cut off – or like a gigantic fuse burning. It lasted about three or four seconds; it did not come from the lamp-post end of "the thing" but it may have come from the other end.

'Vaughan passed me on my left and Clarke, who apparently had understood the shout, also ran towards the building. Realising that I would have to turn right about before I could start running, I crouched down in what is known as prone-falling position number one. Even at that moment I did not imagine that there was any danger in the road, and thought that it was coming from above, up Portland Place. My head was up watching, and before I could reach position number two and lie down flat the thing in the road exploded. I had a momentary glimpse of a large ball of blinding, wild, white light and two concentric rings of colour, the inner one lavender and the outer one violet, as I ducked my head. The ball seemed to be ten to twenty feet high, and was near the lamp-post. Several things happened simultaneously. My head was jerked back due to a heavy blow on the dome and rim of the back of my steel helmet, but I do not remember this, for as my head went back, I received a severe blow on my forehead and the bridge of my nose. The blast bent up the front rim of my helmet and knocked it off my head. The explosion made an indescribable noise – something like a colossal growl – and was accompanied by a veritable tornado of air blast. I felt an excruciating pain in my ears, and all sounds were replaced by a very loud singing noise, which I was told later was when I lost my hearing and had my eardrums

The perils and adversity of the Blitz had a curious effect on the people of Britain, breaking down their natural reserve and building up their defiance

perforated. I felt that consciousness was slipping from me, and that moment I heard a clear loud voice shouting: "Don't let yourself go, face up to it – hold on." It rallied me, and summoning all my willpower and energy I succeeded in forcing myself down into a crouching position with my knees on the ground and my feet against the curb behind me and my hands covering my face.

'I remember having trouble to move them over my ears because of the pain in them, doubtless due to the blast. This seemed to ease the pain. Then I received another hit on the forehead and felt weaker. The blast seemed to come in successive waves, accompanied by vibrations from the ground. I felt as if it were trying to spin me and clear me away from the curb. Then I received a very heavy blow just in front of the right temple which knocked me down flat on my side, in the gutter. Later, in our first-aid post, they removed what they described as a piece of bomb from that wound. Whilst in the gutter I clung on to the curb with both hands and with my feet against it. I was again hit in the right chest, and later found that my double-breasted overcoat, my coat, leather comb-case and papers had been cut through, and the watch in the top right-hand pocket of my waist-coat had the back dented in and its works broken.

'Just as I felt that I could not hold out much longer, I realised that the blast pressure was decreasing and a shower of dust, dirt and rubble swept past me. Pieces penetrated my face, some skin was blown off, and something pierced my left thumbnail and my knuckles were cut, causing me involuntarily to let go my hold on the curb. Instantly, although the blast was dying down, I felt myself being slowly blown across the pavement towards the wall of the building. I tried to hold on but there was nothing to hold on to. Twice I tried to rise but seemed held down. Eventually I staggered to my feet. I looked around and it seemed like a scene from Dante's *Inferno*. The front of the building was lit by a reddish-yellow light; the saloon car was on fire to the left of me, and the flames from it were stretching out towards the building, and not upwards, pieces of brick, masonry and glass seemed to appear on the pavement, making, to me, no sound; a few dark huddled bodies were round about, and right in front of me were two soldiers; one, some feet from a breach in the wall of the building where a fire seemed to be raging, was propped up against the wall with his arms dangling by him, like a rag doll.

'The other was nearer, about twelve feet from the burning car; he was sitting up with his knees drawn up and supporting himself by his arms – his trousers had been blown off him. I could see that his legs were bare and that he was wearing short grey underpants. He was alive and conscious.

'I told him to hang on to an upright at the entrance and to shout like hell for assistance should he see or hear anyone approaching. I went back to look at the other soldier. He was still in the same posture and I fear that he was dead. I looked around. There was a long, dark body lying prone, face downwards close to the curb in front of the building – it may have been Vaughan. There appeared to be one or two dark, huddled bodies by the wall of the building. I had not the strength to lift any of them. I wondered where the water was coming from which I felt dripping down my face, and soon discovered that it was blood from my head wounds. I could see no movement anywhere, and thought I would look round for my steel helmet and gas mask, which I had slung round me at the time of the explosion. I soon found the gas mask and picked up a steel helmet which was not my own.

'I was then joined by my colleague who had returned, and went with him to the entrance where I shouted for assistance for those outside, and for someone to bring fire-fighting appliances to put out the car fire, as I was afraid the glare would bring down more bombs.

'I walked down to our First Aid Post, where I was treated, and then to Listening Hall 1 where I rested until I was taken away by the stretcher party and sent to the Middlesex Hospital. Here I received every possible attention and kindness. Later on I was told that "the thing" had been a land mine, and that its explosion or blast had lasted for nine seconds.

'The effect of the blast on my clothes is possibly of interest, I was wearing bicycle clips round the bottoms of my trousers at the time; after the blast was over my double-breasted overcoat was slit up the back and torn in several places, but was being held together by the belt. My trousers and underpants were pitted with small cuts about an inch long, but presumably the bicycle clips had prevented the draught getting up my trousers and tearing them off. A woollen scarf, which was knotted round my neck, undoubtedly saved my neck and chest from small fragments such as were removed from my face, which was not covered.'

A number of parachute mines did not explode and provided a more obvious and in many ways more terrifying menace than unexploded bombs, since it was known that the proximity of metal, or any sort of vibration, might set them off.

Dealing with unexploded bombs was dangerous enough in all conscience, and the officers and men of the Royal Engineers who carried out this unpleasant duty were much decorated for their bravery. Dealing with unexploded mines, though there was usually no digging to be done before these could be got at, was in many ways just as dangerous, since there was no telling what new fuses and booby-traps the Germans might have built into the monsters. This was normally the duty of the Royal Navy, and Professor Peter Danckwerts, at that time a naval officer who won a

George Cross for neutralising mines in London, has described his experiences as follows:

'In the Blitz of 1940 I was a Bomb Disposal Officer belonging to the Navy and attached to the Port of London. My job was to dispose of bombs which fell in the Port of London area. This wasn't very rewarding because most of the bombs fell in the water and weren't seen, so I didn't have a great deal to do, and I was feeling a little frustrated. Well, one night I was down in the basement of the Port of London Authority building which was a very safe, comfortable place during the Blitz. There was a lot of noise going on outside. The floor was heaving from time to time. The telephone rang and the call was from the air raid controller in a North London borough who said that an object had dropped in a shopping street there, and the local bomb disposal officer thought it might be a magnetic mine. He didn't know, because he'd never seen one, but he wanted to know whether, if he put it on a lorry and took it away, it

was likely to explode. I said I thought it was quite likely to, but it turned out in fact that he'd already done this and taken it away and it hadn't exploded, so he was lucky. Well the next morning I went out with an officer from the Admiralty – I'll call him "R" – who is an expert in mines, to see this thing, and there were also two other mines dropped that night which we were going to see. The first one, which this bomb disposal officer had taken away, was lying in the middle of a big common and it seemed to me an enormous thing. It was eight feet long and about two feet in diameter, thicker than a pillar-box and longer than a tall man. It was dark green and it had a huge parachute spread out behind it, not a silk one – it looked like Aertex or something of that sort. It weighed a ton, it had fifteen hundred pounds of high explosives in it, and it was full of various gadgets which you could see

Troops and workmen remove an unexploded bomb

The Battle of Britain was the first campaign which rammed home Germany's failure to develop a long-range heavy bomber to do the work done by planes such as the HE-111 medium bomber. Like the JU-88, it was also used as an anti-shipping strike aircraft *Crew :* five. *Speed :* 253mph. *Max range :* 1,100 miles. *Bomb load :* 4,000lbs. *Armament :* five 7.92mm machine-guns, one 20mm cannon

let into the side. This was an ordinary magnetic mine of the sort the Germans had been laying in the sea and in the estuaries and harbours of England, but during the Blitz, when a lot of them were dropped, it got to be known as a land mine, although in fact it was just a perfectly ordinary magnetic mine, which went off on land if dropped on land. This officer from the Admiralty, "R", demonstrated to us how the thing should have been dealt with. First of all, in the side, there was a little fuse which was called the bomb fuse. This fuse was supposed to set the mine off if it fell on land and not on water, and he took it out. He had some special tools. It was very stiff, but he took it out and he threw it on the ground, and about ten seconds later there was a crack and the fuse went off. He said that this demonstrated how careful one had to be dealing with these things – if you rolled the mine about a bit with the fuse in it, it was liable to go off. If the mine hit water the bomb fuse didn't function because the mine sank into the water and the pressure of the water pushed in a little pin and stopped it; but when these mines fell

on land, the fuse started buzzing and it buzzed for fifteen seconds, or rather it was supposed to buzz for fifteen seconds and then go off, but some of them buzzed for a few seconds and then stuck, and so if you rolled the mine about it buzzed for the rest of the fifteen seconds and then blew up.

'As "R" said, the important thing when dealing with these mines, if you had to move them at all before you took the fuse out, was to listen very carefully all the time, and if you heard it buzzing to run like hell, because you might have up to fifteen seconds to get away.

'There were a lot of other gadgets in this mine which he showed us how to take out. There was an electric detonator down at the bottom of a hole in the side of the mine which was very hard to get out, since it needed a special shaped tool. Opposite it was another little hole in the mine, and he unscrewed the cover of this and there was a tremendous *whoof* and a spring, three feet long, shot out of it across the field. The other two of us were most alarmed as we hadn't known this was going to happen, but he said: "Well, it's all right, you can come

Maid-of-all-work for the Luftwaffe, serving as dive-bomber, level bomber, night-fighter, and reconnaissance. It also served with distinction in the torpedo-bombing role against Allied convoys. It suffered – like all German bombers – from a chronic weakness in defensive armament. *Crew :* four. Speed: 286mph. *Max range :* 1,553 miles. *Bomb load :* 3,963lbs. *Armament :* four 7.92mm machine-guns

back, this always happens, it's part of the show". And then finally there was a great big screwed-up cover which we eventually managed to get undone, and underneath it was a large clock made of perspex so that you could see the works, and connected to a lot of wires of different colours. This was the clock which, if the mine fell into water, started ticking and after it had ticked for about twenty minutes turned the thing into a magnetic mine So we took that out, and cut the wires, and then the thing was quite safe.

'Then we went off and looked at the other two. One of them had fallen on a little house while the family were having supper. They were sitting in the kitchen, and there was a tremendous uproar from the scullery, great crashings, a lot of slates falling and so on. They had tried to get in the scullery to see what had happened, but couldn't, so they went out of the front door and round at the back door of the scullery, and then they found this mine standing up against the back of the scullery door. It was still there when we got there and the supper was still on the table.

'Well, after this demonstration I

went back and I took a fuse from one of these mines with me. I worked on it and took it to bits that evening with a torpedo officer, who was working in the Port of London at that time, and we reckoned we knew pretty well how it worked. This was just as well, because in the course of that night we got another telephone call, this time from South London, to say that three large objects on parachutes had dropped in their particular area. The local Army bomb disposal officer said this was a job for the Navy because he thought they were mines, and the ARP Controller wanted to know what I was going to do about it. I said that actually I wasn't supposed to deal with mines at all, but only with bombs. He said: "Oh, my God, who does deal with mines?" I said: "I'm afraid that the nearest people are down in Portsmouth." He said: "That's all very well, but I've got several thousand people evacuated round these mines, I can't wait for the people to come up from Portsmouth." So I rang up HMS *Vernon* at Portsmouth, which is the torpedo and mining school down there, and asked the duty officer whether I could go and deal with these mines.

I said I thought I knew how to do it, and he reluctantly said yes. So I went and woke up the torpedo officer who'd been playing with the fuse with me, and my Chief Petty Officer, who was another torpedo-man, both of them very good with gadgets and getting difficult things unscrewed and so on. Of course we didn't have any of the proper tools for this job. (One was supposed to have non-magnetic tools, quite apart from which most of the things were very hard to unscrew unless you had tools of the right shape.) But we got a lot of screwdrivers and, most important of all, we took a ball of string, that is the essential thing for bomb disposal.

'Well, we set off, in a car we had got from the Admiralty, and we drove through the Blitz. It was a horrible night. We drove round craters and wrecked trams and blazing gas mains, past anti-aircraft batteries which were bang-banging away. We had an imperturbable driver, I was full of admiration for him, but eventually we got down into the wilds of South London and of course we got lost. We didn't know where we were, we didn't know where any of the three mines we were looking for was either. We were wandering around back streets with shrapnel coming down and not getting any closer, and it wasn't till we saw a man in a dressing-gown walking along with a suitcase that we felt we might be getting warm. So we stopped him and asked him, and he said: Oh yes, it had fallen in the garden of a house near his. So we made him come back with us and show us. We went into the back garden of this little house. This was our first mine, and we saw it lying there among the bushes, a parachute spread over the wall next door. We went up and had a look at it with our torch, and we found unfortunately that the all-important fuse was underneath, so we'd have to roll it round before we could get it out. My Chief Petty Officer and I rolled it over very, very cautiously indeed while the third member of the party

kept his ear as close to it as he could and listened to see if it buzzed. It didn't. So when we'd got the fuse round to the side, we unscrewed it. But we didn't take it out because the Germans had on occasions put things under fuses in bombs so that when you took the fuse out the bomb blew up, and it was quite possible to do it in these mines as well. Having unscrewed it, when it was loose in its socket, we tied a bit of string to the top and then we retired over the garden wall into the next garden, and then over the next garden wall into the garden beyond that, and then round the corner of the house, paying out the string, and when we got there I gave a yank on the string. It seemed sort of elastic, and when I let go the string sprang back again, so we had to climb all the way back and look. Of course the string was tied up with a rose bush or something. We freed it, and then went back and had another pull, and that was all right – when we got back we found the fuse was lying on the ground. I took off the exploder and it was then quite safe. But I did just try throwing it a few yards and sure enough, it fired, it went off, so the thing was still in a fairly sensitive condition, and we were quite right to have treated it with respect.

'I think about twenty per cent of the mines that were dropped didn't go off, and each one that was dropped meant the evacuation of perhaps a thousand people in some cases. The importance of these mines to the Navy was that each one of them was likely to be a perfectly good magnetic mine, with inside it a complete magnetic mine unit, which was capable of sinking a ship if the mine had been laid in the sea. So the Navy were extremely keen on getting as many of these as they could, because they had to follow the development of German magnetic mines in order to develop their counter-measures. The Navy naturally took steps to stop anybody except people whom they felt they could trust not to blow themselves up from dealing with these mines, because they wanted the things intact. We found ourselves eventually officially accredited mine disposal officers.

'There is a tailpiece to this story. In 1945, when the German forces surrendered, I met a colonel of the Luftwaffe and had a long technical talk with him. He had been in charge of the design of airborne mines at one time, and I asked him why they dropped magnetic mines in London as bombs, without any attempt to drop them in the river or in the docks? Why had they just scattered them over London as perfectly ordinary bombs? He said: "It was that Luftwaffe staff. I had a frightful time with them. I tried to stop them. I pointed out that these had been designed as mines to sink ships, and not as bombs to blow up houses, but they wouldn't listen. All they wanted was something with the biggest possible bang to try and demoralise England. They were trying to finish the war off quickly and we didn't manage to stop them dropping them on land." So it may be some comfort that at least every one of these mines that was dropped on London probably meant one less hazard to ships in our harbours and estuaries, and thus made some contribution to winning the Battle of the Atlantic.'

Nobody knew what might not next fall from the skies. There were vague rumours, which I remember hearing at the time, of a most monstrous 'radium bomb', a faint echo of pre-war researches into nuclear fission. Other rumours, which seemed more credible then, were equally unfounded, even though these were on occasion given the authenticity of Government authority. Thus early in November an ARP notice was sent out to wardens which said: "Tins of toffees are believed to have been dropped by enemy aeroplanes. They are shaped like handbags, and some have a coloured tartan design, with puzzle, on the lid, marked Lyons' Assorted Toffee and *"Skotch"*, bearing the name J Lyons & Co., Ltd,

N.14, or Cadby Hall, London. Any found to be handed immediately to police, stating where found with time and date.' Needless to say, none of these diabolical contraptions ever was found, and the origin of the rumour is unfortunately lost in obscurity.

Mr Mallet, who in 1940 was living in Chelsea – 'carting X-ray equipment for the hospitals' is his own description of his job – was a fire-watcher. He has said how people at his post were always discussing strange and weird bombs. One new weapon of which he heard tell contained a huge coil spring, like the spring inside a gramophone, '. . . and if you got in the way of this thing, they said that it'd either cut your legs off, or your head off, or cut you in half. You just laugh at things like that at the time, you think they're talking out of the back of their neck, you don't take any more notice of it. But those things flash through your mind later on.' One windy night, during a raid, he was down by the Chelsea Old Church. 'They was dropping different things all over London again. Presently I heard something come down and go with a dull thud. It may have gone in the river, I don't know. Then I heard this noise.' It was a strange, scraping, metallic sound, which seemed to be coming closer in the semi-darkness. 'Well, immediately I heard this noise it reminded me of what they were saying about this coil spring. I didn't stop to look, I just took to my heels and started to go. I went up Church Street as far and as fast as I could. All I could see was the houses on either side of me, and I didn't even bother to look whether any doors were open or not.' Because, as he started up Old Church Street, he had realised that this thing, this noise, was following him, rattling and scraping along the street just about as fast as he could run. It was, indeed, gaining on him. 'I just belted hell for leather up the road. I thought, this darned thing, whatever it is, it can't turn round a

Left: The inevitable cup of tea, England's cure for all ills. *Above:* The Wardens' Post, nerve centre of London's civilian defences

corner surely. So when I got to Paultons Street I turned the corner, and as I did this thing went by me. It stopped up the road about a hundred yards further on.' He saw it, in the half light, a dome-shaped object in the centre of the road. For some minutes he waited at the corner of the street, ready to dodge back should it show any sign of life. After a little while curiosity won, and he made his way cautiously towards it. 'And when I got up to it, what I found was this bloody dustbin lid that had chased me up the road.' And, Mr Mallet added, when he told me this story: 'You can laugh at it now, but by Christ you never did then.'

When the raids started the Germans had two principal incendiary weapons. One was the oil-bomb, a large drum of oil with an explosive fuse which scattered the burning contents for several yards in all directions. This was a clumsy and not very effective fire-raiser, and was later abandoned.

The other was the thermite incendiary. This was about a foot and a half in length and weighed only a couple of pounds, so that a bomber plane could carry thousands of them. By the time they reached the ground their momentum was enough to take them through a normal tiled or slate roof, and they would then burn furiously, the magnesium alloy container fusing on impact. Sometimes they were simply poured out through the bomb-bays: sometimes they were held in aluminium containers which exploded near to the ground, thus scattering the incendiaries over a comparatively small area. Sir Aylmer Firebrace, Chief of the Fire Staff with London Region during the Blitz, has written in his book *Fire Service Memories:*

'It was a strange experience to be in the centre of a concentration of IBs. One moment the street would be dark, the next it would be illuminated by a hundred sizzling blueish-white flames. They made a curious plop-plopping sound as they fell on roads and pavements, but this was not often heard above the shrill whirring noise made by the pumps. They never gave me the impression that they had been dropped from the skies – they seemed rather to have sprouted.'

When first they landed they were quite easily smothered, with sand, a sandbag, or almost anything else to hand: they could even be picked up with a pair of tongs or heavy gloves, dropped in an empty bucket and carried away to a safe place, while in a roadway or on a stone roof they could usually be safely left to burn themselves out.

But in December the Germans began dropping incendiaries with a small explosive charge in the nose which exploded when the heat reached it. A man or woman who was then dealing with one of the things would be badly hurt, perhaps blinded, perhaps killed. From then on about one in ten of the incendiaries dropped contained this small explosive charge, but of course all of them were potential grenades and had to be treated as such. Dealing with them became far more perilous, and if they were not dealt with at once, they would soon start a blaze.

Every night of the raids there were fires, though until late December none approached the magnitude of the huge docks fire which had started the Blitz. In a blacked-out house, the occupants of which were in a shelter, an incendiary bomb that had come through the roof would often not be seen, nor the fire detected, behind the black-out curtains, until the upper floor was thoroughly ablaze. This happened frequently to warehouses and office buildings, locked up for the night and deserted, and was partly responsible for the huge City fire of late December.

The great fire raid of December 29th was not, from the German point of view, a particularly large-scale operation. Only 136 bombers were over the target, and they dropped 127 tons of high explosive and 613 canisters of incendiaries. In five previous raids on London (and in nine provincial raids) greater weights of incendiaries had been dropped: on 15th November 1,412 canisters of incendiaries had des-

cended on London, and on 8th December, 3,188, or over five times the weight dropped on to the City three weeks later. Nor was the target deliberately chosen: the X-beams which guided the leading bombers of KG 100 over London intersected a couple of miles further to the west. But it was the City that caught the weight of the attack, and in particularly difficult circumstances.

This was a Sunday evening, the end of Christmas week. Despite appeals by the Government, many City office blocks and warehouses were securely locked against burglars, and many of these had no fire-watchers to put out the incendiaries as soon as they landed. Almost all the churches were also locked up and unguarded, with the notable exception of St Paul's Cathedral. The City that was still standing on the afternoon of 29th December 1940, consisted, apart from some of its churches and the halls of the City Companies, entirely of buildings erected after the middle of the nineteenth century. The modern ferro-concrete blocks, of which there were few, were usually immune to the direct action of the incendiaries, which burned out harmlessly upon their flat roofs. The late Victorian and Edwardian buildings, on the other hand, with pitched roofs of slate or glass, caught easily and quickly. And there was a westerly wind blowing at some fifty miles an hour to fan the flames.

So the firemen found themselves confronted, very soon, with a vast number of fires, many of which were quite inaccessible. And then the water failed. The emergency main from the Thames to the Grand Junction Canal, a 24-inch underground pipe constructed just before the war, and running through the City, was broken by high explosive bombs. The sheer number of pumps operating caused the pressure drawn from other sources to drop to nothing, in many individual pumps the jet fading away quite quickly to a mere trickle. The few static water tanks then existing were soon drained dry. And the Thames that evening was at such an abnormally low ebb that its saving waters were out of reach to most of the pumps installed on its embankments and bridges. Little use could be made of fireboats: some were immobilised, downstream of the Tower Bridge, by an unexploded parachute mine, while one of the very few in a position to supply water collided with a submerged wreck and was temporarily out of action.

The raid was a short one. It began a little before seven and lasted only a couple of hours. (The Germans had intended to come back later, to stoke up the fires, but the weather closing in over their bomber bases mercifully made this impossible.) By the time they had gone, there were almost fifteen hundred fires burning, some in Shoreditch, Finsbury and Stepney, but over 1,400 in the City. Many of these quickly joined up to produce two huge conflagrations, one of about a quarter of a square mile, centred around Fore Street, which was simply left to burn itself out, and one twice this size which consumed everything between Moorgate, Aldersgate Street, Cannon Street and Old Street and which produced the biggest area of war devastation in all Britain. On the edge of this greater area stood St Paul's, where perhaps the most famous photograph of the Blitz was taken by Mr Herbert Mason on this night. It shows the dome of St Paul's rising majestically above the swirling pink and black clouds of smoke. Mr Mason has described what he then saw in these words:

'I remember only too well the night of the 29th December, a Sunday night. Shortly after the alert it was obvious that the City was the target for the night. It wasn't long before incendiaries were coming down like rain. Within an hour or so the whole of the City seemed to be lighting up. In the near foreground buildings were blazing furiously and it wasn't long before the Wren church of St Bride's was a mass of flames. The famous wedding-cake steeple was being licked. In the distance through the smoke you could see the fires increasing, and as the evening wore on an artificial wind sprang through the heat caused by the fires, parted the clouds, the buildings in the foreground collapsed, and there revealed in all its majesty was St Paul's, a hauntingly beautiful picture which no artist could recapture. Down below in the street I went towards Ludgate Hill, which was carpeted in hose pipes, a scampering rat here and there, a reeling bird in the flames. The heat became intense as I approached St Paul's Churchyard. Firemen were fighting a losing battle. Pathetically little water was coming from their hoses. Suddenly a fresh supply would come and a hose running riot would lash out and knock firemen from their feet. The heat was so intense that embers were falling like rain and clattering on your helmet. Cheapside was a mass of flames, leaping from one side of the road to the other.

'Back at my vantage point on top of the *Daily Mail* building, where I was, I could see that this night I was going to obtain the picture which would for ever record the Battle of Britain. After waiting a few hours the smoke parted like the curtain of a theatre and there before me was this wonderful vista, more like a dream, not frightening – there were very few high explosives. It was obvious that this was going to be the second Great Fire of London. The tragedy of this second great fire of London was the fact that there were so few fire-watchers. Single handed I could have prevented thousands of pounds' worth of damage being done, but the buildings were locked, there was nobody present to force an entry. There were so few people. It was pathetic.'

Eight Wren churches went that night as well as the Guildhall which, however, had been so thoroughly restored in the eighteen-sixties that

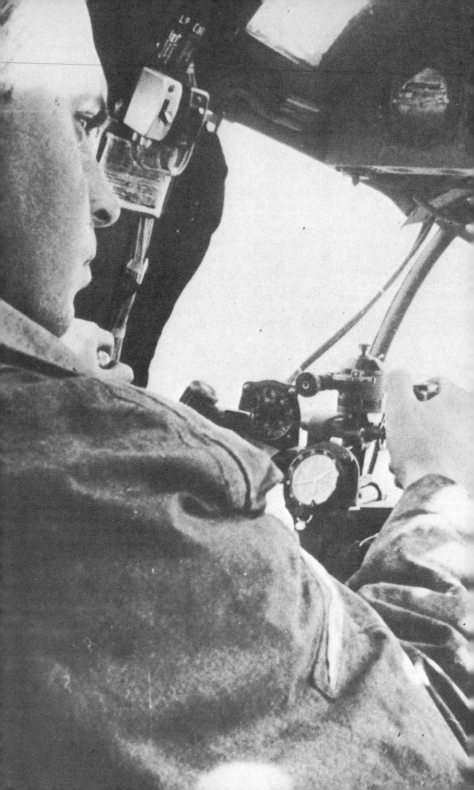

Bomb aimer in the nose of an He-111
medium bomber

He-111s in formation over England

this was more a sentimental than an architectural tragedy. Guy's Hospital was licked by flames and had to be evacuated. The Central Telegraph Office, the GPO telecommunications plant and three City telephone exchanges were put out of action. Five railway stations and sixteen underground stations were closed.

But St Paul's was saved. A watcher across the river in Lambeth saw this:

'An unforgettable sight. The whole of London seemed involved, one great circle of overwhelming disaster, save in one corner where the night sky was clear. One could not distinguish buildings through the great clouds of smoke, except when there was a sudden spurt of yellow flames which lit up a church tower, and it seemed impossible that the City, that London could be saved. There was only that one bit of calm sky in the distance as a symbol of hope that the circle would not be completed.'

That clear patch of sky was above the Cathedral, which at least one over-anxious American correspondent had already reported destroyed to his newspaper. Indeed, it seemed in-credible that it should survive.

Twenty-eight incendiaries landed on St Paul's that night, and watchers on the roof of the *Daily Telegraph* building say that a veritable cascade of them was seen to hit the dome and bounce off. The dome is, in fact, a double dome, and between the outer dome, visible from the street – or from the air – and the inner, which floats above the nave, there is a hollow space containing dry old beams, and almost inaccessible. Had any incendiaries penetrated the skin of lead that is the outer dome, the Cathedral must have been almost certainly burned down.

Hundreds of feet above the burning City the men of the St Paul's Cathedral Watch, clerics and laymen attached to the chapter as well as many volunteers, often architects, who had chosen to do this duty, fought the incendiaries. Almost at once the water supply failed, but luckily the foresighted leaders of the Watch, Dr Allen and Mr Linge, had insisted on supplies of reserve water, tanks, baths, even pails of water, being scattered throughout the structure. With this water and with stirrup pumps, the Cathedral was saved. It was not easy.

Bombs which had lodged in the roof timbers were particularly dangerous and hard to tackle. Some burned for three quarters of an hour, though simultaneously tackled by two squads one above and one below.

But the most dangerous incendiary of all was out of reach. It had struck the dome perpendicular to its surface and was lodged halfway through the outer shell. Though the dome was not actually burning, the bomb was blazing, the lead about it was melting, no man could reach it, and it seemed only a matter of minutes before it must fall inside the dome, among the beams and other dry timber. As the Dean has said: 'We knew that once a fire got hold of the dome timbers it would, at that high altitude, quickly be fanned into a roaring furnace . . .' And then, suddenly, as the men who loved the Cathedral waited and watched for what seemed the inevitable catastrophe an extraordinarily thing happened. The bomb fell outwards, landing on the Stone Gallery where it was quickly and easily extinguished.

Though the Chapter House, the Dean's Verger's House, the Organist's House – all very close to the Cathedral – were burned out and one of the Minor Canons' houses was seriously damaged, the Cathedral emerged from this night of inferno almost unscathed

To many it seemed a sort of miracle. St Paul's, during that winter, had simply and majestically taken its rightful place as London's church. A theatrical producer has told this writer that every morning, after a raid, he would look first from the windows of his Hampstead flat towards the City, to make sure that the great dome still stood. And a simple woman in Bethnal Green, the one who, when the raids started, 'donned her helmet and out she went', remembers the night of the City blaze as follows:

'I went up on the roof with some of the firemen, to look at the City. And I've always remembered how I was choked, I think I was crying a little. I could see St Paul's standing there, and the fire all around, and I just said: 'Please God, don't let it go!' I couldn't help it, I felt that if St Paul's had gone, something would have gone from us. But it stood in defiance, it did. And when the boys were coming back, the firemen said: "It's bad, but, oh, the old church stood it." Lovely, that was.'

One night in Chelsea

The great City fire had revealed beyond dispute the inadequacy of the fire-prevention and fire-fighting arrangements. The Government was taken aback, and in January new regulations were passed which gave the Minister powers to compel persons of both sexes within certain age limits to carry out part-time civil defence duties. Men between the ages of sixteen and sixty had to register, and were ordered to do up to forty-eight hours per month duty as firewatchers: this order was later extended to women. Another regulation laid down that business premises must be guarded and supplied with firefighting equipment.

This marked a fundamental change to the nature of civil defence. Hitherto largely a voluntary matter, it now became more and more an affair of conscripts. So far as the prevention of fire went the new arrangements were very successful. Though they tried, the Germans never again succeeded in setting fire to any large area of London.

The arrangements for emergency water supplies were also thoroughly overhauled, great quantities of hose and transportable canvas dams being made available and large numbers of static water tanks built into the basements of the demolished buildings. Later the whole Fire Service was to be nationalised.

The more active defences also made considerable progress during the comparative lull, from mid-January to early March. A German pilot has said that he realised, with considerable apprehension, that anti-aircraft shells were exploding near his aircraft when he was actually flying in cloud. This, he realised at once, meant that the guns were now being equipped with radar.

But it was the night fighter that really made the most progress during the first few months of 1941. The mounting successes of this arm can be ascribed to the growing skill of the pilots and navigators, and to the much greater efficiency of the radar installations, both airborne and on the ground. The system, in essence, was that the ground radar detected the enemy bomber and ground control guided the night fighter towards him until the fighter's own radar set could pick up the enemy. The fighter would then close to within visual range, perhaps two or three hundred feet, identify the enemy, and shoot him down. This required a very high degree of skill on the part of the pilot and navigator and split-second organisation on the part of ground control. These were achieved, and from mid-March on, according to a German bomber pilot, the night fighters became far more of a menace to the enemy than the guns. Indeed, he has said, when pursued by a night fighter he would deliberately fly into the gun zone, or even in among the barrage balloons, to shake off his pursuer.

Searchlights probe for bombers over London

One of London's worst-hit areas, the City in the vicinity of St Paul's Cathedral. Great damage was caused, but few people lived in the district

These dark battles – the detection of the enemy, the stealthy approach in the night sky, the sudden burst of cannon fire from sharp astern, and, with luck, the disintegration of the enemy – took place far out of sight of London's weary millions. The news of the successes of the night fighters was nonetheless extremely heartening to the tired people on the ground. In January and February the night fighters had shot at only 9 bombers per month: in March the figure was 25: in April 34: and in May 116, a startling increase.

The civilian population needed encouragement, for though the raids on London were few after the lull, some of them were exceptionally vicious and violent.

On 8th March 125 planes bombed the capital: on 9th March, 94: and on the 15th, 101. These raids were comparable in weight to those of the Christmas period. But the four further raids that London was to suffer that spring were the heaviest of all. On 19th March, 479 bombers dropped 467 tons of HE and 3,347 incendiary canisters: on 16th April, 'the Wednesday', 685 planes dropped 890 tons of HE and 4,200 canisters of incendiaries: three nights later, 'the Saturday', came the heaviest raid of all, with 712 planes dropping 1,026 tons of HE and 4,252 incendiary canisters: and on 10th May, London's last, 507 planes dropped 711 tons of HE and 2,393 incendiary canisters.

When it is realised that only once during the autumn – on 15th October – had the enemy dropped more than 400 tons of HE in a night, the ferocity of these later raids becomes self-evident. The especial savagery of the Wednesday and the Saturday is explicable in that these were specifically ordered by Hitler, as reprisals for the bombing of Berlin, and he had laid down that they were to be as heavy as possible. Many German aircrews flew two, and some flew three, sorties on those nights. And the bombs dropped were now much heavier, the incendiaries more efficient.

Though the civil defence services were highly experienced and most competently trained by now, the sheer weight of these last four massive attacks seems almost to have overwhelmed the ground defence. Had the Germans launched attacks on this scale at the beginning of the Blitz, or had they carried out sustained and repeated attacks on this scale in April and May, there is some doubt as to whether London could have endured them without at least a drastic revision of the whole system of shelters, evacuation and defence. But luckily they were few, they were spaced, and London was given time to recover between these tremendous punches; for this was the time when the Luftwaffe was doing its best to smash the provincial cities as well. (It must not, however, be imagined that the weight of attack on the provincial towns was in any way comparable to that on London. London, which had received some 19,000 tons of bombs before 14th November, had over 5,000 more tons, in fourteen raids, after that date. No other target was bombed more than eight times, or received as much as 2,000 tons of bombs.)

Since by April the move of the German armies to the Eastern Front had already begun, these last, heavy raids were in no wise a preliminary to invasion. It may be asked why the Germans carried out these murderous attacks. One explanation may be that Hitler hoped that his 'reprisal' raids would cause the British Government to reconsider their own bombing policy: a more likely one is that these raids, by concentrating the attention of the world on the British Isles, were intended to mask the move of the armies to the East, that they were in fact part of a vast cover plan: a third, and also probable, explanation is that even at this late stage Hitler and Göring still hoped that it might be possible to knock Britain out of the war by air attack alone, thus giving the Wehrmacht a free hand in the East: and finally, violent air operations of this sort undoubtedly appealed to Hitler's sadistic nature. In any event, brutal as they were, the attacks failed to achieve any of their objectives save possibly that of masking the forthcoming Eastern Campaign from the Russians.

But brutal they certainly were, and the strain on the men and women of the Civil Defence Service, already very tired after the long autumn and winter, was great. But it cannot be stressed too strongly that the brunt of the battle of London was borne by the firemen, and perhaps even more so by the wardens. For an accurate picture of how they worked, here is a description of a major incident of the Wednesday raid. For this I am indebted to Mr L W Matthews, a Post Warden of D Post in Chelsea, who was directly concerned in the event described, the bombing of the Chelsea Old Church.

On the night of 16–17th April 1941, almost 700 German bombers attacked South and Central London for nearly eight hours. Civilian casualties were over 1,000 killed and 2,000 seriously injured, and among the buildings hit were 18 hospitals and 13 churches, one of which was Chelsea Old Church.

Owing perhaps to its position on the river and proximity to the centre of Government, the power stations and similar objectives, Chelsea had already suffered considerable damage. Taking its size into account, it was one of the most heavily bombed boroughs in London, only Holborn and Shoreditch receiving a heavier tonnage of bombs per acre. On the nights we are concerned with, five parachute mines, a number of other high-explosive bombs and many hundreds of incendiaries fell within Chelsea's boundaries, in an area of about 660 acres.

Chelsea Old Church was guarded by a party of volunteers from the congregation and nearby business premises.

Try to see this area as it was then, with sparse wartime traffic accelerating in the main thoroughfares as the sirens' wailing rose and fell, warning and challenging. Doors were opening and shutting in all the darkened streets as people left home for the shelters in Paultons Square, the Rectory Garden or the Embankment Gardens. Street Fire Parties met and looked up at the sky, already throbbing with approaching bombers.

Wardens were converging on the wardens' post, to join those on duty. They came blinking from a dark corridor into the small classroom, reduced in height and space by steel joints supporting heavy baulks of timber overhead, helmeted and dungareed men and women hampered by the respirators, hooded lamps, belts hung with pouches containing report pads, axes, extra torches and first-aid packs. As patrols were paired off and dispatched to report on the numbers of persons occupying shelters and the state of manning of fire party posts, a pattern of routine emerged. Messages were exchanged with the Control Centre under the Town Hall, with other wardens' posts and with the warden posted as look-out on the roof of the school. Those not detailed for a duty settled down in deck chairs to read, write or chat over a cup of tea.

The telephone rang: the rooftop look-out reported parachute flares dropping in the south-east, and a few minutes later over Lots Road Power Station. A patrol came back with the numbers of people sheltering in the Embankment Gardens shelters and the state of the fire parties in that sector. Another patrol had nothing to report but mentioned that bombs were falling across the river in Battersea and fires had been started to the south and south-east.

At half past nine the Post Warden left his deputy in charge and went out

on a cycle patrol of the area. In spite of the noise of gunfire and aircraft it was quiet enough, cycling slowly in the middle of the road, for him to hear the swish of the tyres, the occasional tinkle of falling shell casing. On returning to the school he climbed many stairs, past floor after floor of deserted classrooms to the flat roof.

Downstairs in the post a fresh brew of tea was waiting.

At half past eleven the roof look-out reported a heavy explosion and clouds of black smoke in the eastern half of Chelsea, near the river. This was not in Post Don's area and no action was called for. They learned through an adjacent post that the Royal Hospital Infirmary had been hit and the AFS station at 21 Cheyne Place put out of action. There were many casualties and widespread damage, due apparently to a single heavy bomb. There were rumours that part of a 'landmine' had been found.

By one in the morning about forty ʼapped casualties had been reported t the Royal Hospital Infirmary. A ardens' post nearby had dealt with ore than that number of walking ses and homeless persons. Nothing ad fallen in the Post Don's area. The ost Warden was conducting his nior officer, the District Warden, n a tour of the area, and they were turning from watching incendiary mbs rattling down on warehouse ofs across the river when they saw e six members of the Old Church re Party leave the shadow of the wer and walk away from it along eyne Walk towards Danvers Street. The Post Warden had returned to ok's Ground School and was just tting down to make an entry in the g Book, when two heavy explo- ons occurred close at hand. The me was twenty past one. Everything the room jumped, dust was shaken wn, the sound of breaking glass and

Hard men and strong rope demolish a badly damaged building

splintering woodwork came from else- where in the building. Leaving the telephonist in charge of the Post, the Post Warden despatched all available wardens to investigate and went out himself. The District Warden joined him in the corridor. His windows had been blown in on top of him as he sat in his office, but he had escaped injury.

As they turned the corner from Glebe Place into Upper Cheyne Row lights were visible in some of the houses; windows and window frames complete with blackout had been sucked out into the road or pushed into the room. Tiles, broken slates, lath and plaster, bits of wood and glass littered the roadway, but this was only minor damage.

Justice Walk was blocked half way in from Lawrence Street, and it was

133

evident that the centre of damage was somewhere on the other side of it.

As they ran round the corner into Cheyne Walk they were brought down by a length of garden railing. They saw flames leaping up in a thinning dust haze. Near Danvers Street in a shallow crater in the road a gas main was on fire. And then it came to them both: 'The Old Church has gone!' There was a jagged stump of brickwork and projecting timbers silhouetted where the eye had expected the massive square tower.

Some of the houses beyond it in Cheyne Walk were demolished, others were hanging shells, blasted through from back to front. A woman was calling for help from one of them. Leaving the District Warden to organise what help was available on the spot, the Post Warden ran back to the Post to send the brief message which would bring the necessary casualty services. The telephonist at Control Centre repeated the message back to him: 'Post Don. Express Report. Chelsea Old Church. Trapped Casualties. Fire. Time of reference 0125 hours. Message Ends.' It was now his duty to collect various paraphernalia, blue hat cover, blue lamps, portable desk complete with log and message pads, and to assume the role of Incident Officer at the 'Incident', for that was what the Old Church had now become.

On his return to the Incident the Post Warden's first task was to estimate the extent of the damage and numbers and position of trapped casualties. A quick reconnaissance over the rubble gave him his bearings. Church Street was blocked a good way up. He sent a report by runner that all vehicles must approach by Cheyne Walk. The Express Report would automatically bring a Rescue Party, Stretcher Party and Ambulance; reinforcements would probably be needed.

The Church itself was no more than a great heap of rubble and broken timbers. The blast had lifted the old bricks and blown out the powder mortar like a winnowing fan: no much point in looking for anyone i that. The first house in Petyt Plac had been demolished, but the others though ripped open, still stood, an lights showed in one of them. A ma with a minor wound was given firs aid. Other wardens were detailed t search all damaged houses in th vicinity.

Behind the ruins of the Church th end wall of the nurses' home of th Cheyne Hospital for Children ros undamaged to about two thirds u the second floor: there the brickwor had been sucked away along a clea line from back to front, leaving th top floor exposed in section from th floor joists to the roof space. Ther was a made-up bed, a chair, an ope wardrobe and a ceiling light sti burning. With a gas main alight jus round the corner, there was little poin in worrying about infringements of the blackout regulations, but fro force of habit one of the searchin wardens climbed perilously up th exposed staircase, now supported onl on one side, and switched it off.

An eerie hallooing in the cavernou darkness of one of the damage Cheyne Walk houses seemed t promise the whereabout of casualtie but turned out to be a policema engaged in a search on his own.

The warden in charge of parkin arrangements came up to report tha no ambulances had arrived, but th Rescue and Stretcher parties arrive and a search began for other resident of the little houses who, according t the wardens' census records, we missing. A gap in the pavemer giving off a heavy odour of town ga suggested a way in, but proved impa sable until a very small Rescue ma the others called 'Yorkie' wriggle through and searched what was i fact an empty cellar. Some of th men began tunnelling into the wrec

St Paul's, still standing amid the ruins of the City

age: others began working at 77 Cheyne Walk, the *New Café Lombard,* where it was feared some of the fire party might be trapped with another party of three known to be posted there. The body of a man who might be one of them but had not been identified had been found by the bus stop across the road.

Someore came up with the news that one of the fire party had escaped and was now at his home at 27 Old Church Street. It was important to find out what had happened to the others, and handing over to a deputy, the Post Warden went to find Arthur Mallett.

He was lying on a couch in the darkened, blitzed ground-floor back room with other members of the family huddled round him. He had had an almost miraculous escape, and was the only survivor of the little party of fire-watchers:

'This precise evening I was there, there was the crowd of us all around in the fire-watching post down in Petyt House, Old Church Street, just down by the old Chelsea church. When the alert went, we all don our tin hats and everything, helmets, gas-masks we had with us, some were old ex-Army ones, I know, but anyhow, we had them all strapped on to us and away we go, down on to the embankment. When we get down there there's a hell of a lot of shrapnel and stuff coming down, I think they let everything fly. So I'm standing there, all of a sudden something comes down beside me, a big lump of shrapnel or something, so I went over, picked it up and I looked at it and I said to myself: "Christ," I said, "this is expensive metal to be throwing about." And I was looking, then I see it was where the nose-cap had rubbed over the piece of shrapnel and made it look as if it was phosphorous bronze. So being disillusioned, about not making any money out of it, I just was going to dump it. But that second there was such a thud at the side of me, like a fifty-six pound coal-sack dropping on

the soft ground. I didn't take a lot notice, I was still looking at this pie of metal, I was just going to throw away again, and then I looked: "(Christ," I said like that to myself looked, there was this big cylind laying down beside me. I could ha picked it up. Anyhow, I turned rou to the other firewatchers, I said: "F Christ's sake, run!" Anyhow they ru they was about twenty feet farth away than where I was. Anyho they run towards Chelsea Old Churc even then I didn't run, I stood the and I thought: "Well, I don't kno it's about time I got cracking." see them running, I had no more do, I started to run. Well, as I near the bottom of Old Church Street I s up such a speed that I couldn't tu the corner. I thought: "Bugger th so right ho, I'll carry straight or Anyhow, there was a little iron po and a fire post down beside the (church, it was about the only coverir and I thought: "Well, this post stuck in the ground well, that wo move in a hurry." So I crouched do beside that. Well, as it happened the must have been another land mi come down behind the church. As did so it exploded and blew the c

The remains of Chelsea Old Church Street

off that I'd already left. Well, the next thing I remember was – I looked, and when I looked, I couldn't see anything. And I thought: "Well, I don't know, the eyes have gone," and it put the wind up me for the minute. But I just sat there, closed me eyes again, I looked up in the air, I thought: "Well, I'm bound to see stars." There were a few out, so I looked up, I looked up, I see millions of them, but they wasn't stars. It was as if I'd been hit on the head with something and you're sort of dazed. So I sort of crouched down again, sat there for a few minutes more, I suppose, it seemed like hours, but I just sat there, and when I looked up again I see a little bright one in among the lot, so I thought: "Ah, that's all right, I am all right." Anyhow, when I got up I found half me trousers had gone, that was me trousers on me right leg. Then I felt something running down me left leg. I thought; "I'm not looking at that." So I stood up for a few minutes and then I could see why it was I couldn't see. There was so much dust and that flying around that I was completely blacked out. Well, I turned round to look up Old Church Street, naturally, because I live up there.

When I looked I couldn't see anything – it looked just like a mountain of rubble. "Blimey," I thought, "that lot's gone." And when I came up Old Church Street I went indoors and I went to lay down on the bed, the next thing happens, the Chief Warden comes round, he wanted to know what happened. Well, I was too fed up to answer him, all I wanted to do was to get to sleep and get to work, so I near enough told him where to go, straight away, and I went indoors and lay down for a couple of hours. Well, I felt so rough and dirty and that, that I was on this work at the time, I was carting X-ray equipment for the hospitals, so I thought: "Well, there's only one place I know where they might have some tea, and that's at the Fulham Road workhouse, or institution as they call it now." So I had no more to do, I went up there, and I knew Mr Bentall the baker, I went down to see him, so he said: "Hello, Bill," he said, "what's the matter with you?" So I said: "Well," I said, "they've just blown Chelsea Old Church up," I said, "made a bit of a mess down there," I said. So he said, "What do you want?" I said, "I want a cup of tea first off." Anyhow, he comes back with a big pint mug of tea, and I think that's the best pint of tea that I've ever had in my life.'

Mr Matthews returned to the scene of the disaster. He has written:

'The ambulance station at Blanche's Garage was out of commission. Trapped casualties were now estimated at ten. Another stretcher had been sent for.

'In the debris of number six Old Church Street the Rescue men had reached Emma Chandler, aged sixteen. Her face had been uncovered and she was talking normally to the man beside her. The Rescue Party Leader explained that she was trapped by joists jammed by heavy masonry. Each piece would have to be sawn through and shored up, with the constant possibility of everything subsiding into the cellar below. There was a powdering of ochreous dust over the torch-lit group. However carefully they worked, there was a continuous rattle of particles among the debris.'

Mr Matthews has amplified what he has written about that night, in these words:

'Perhaps I ought to try and paint a more precise picture of the incident. By this time there was a big pile of debris, the rubble at the bottom of Old Church Street, right across the roadway. We had to climb, scramble over it and all sorts of holes and craters in it. I remember my own wrists were grazed from it and we were continually falling into the holes, it wasn't at all the sort of textbook method of conducting an incident. We had to find each other to begin with. We had torches but they quite often got broken. We had a method of keeping a record of the incident, a sort of rough log on a piece of paper on a board which was fastened round our necks on a dog lead, but of course falling into holes, dropping it, you had to carry the thing in your head

most of the time. But there was this pile of debris and beside it, just a little way up Church Street on the right-hand side where the rubble of the cottages was, the rescue party were working. I don't think they needed very much light because there was a good deal of general light on the scene, but there were hooded torches and in the middle of the party, the men who were working, there was this girl trapped, and of course they had to work very carefully, because if they'd gone at it too roughly the debris would have collapsed on her. The work could only go on very slowly there. Just a little way across the road, in Petyt Place, the houses were rather badly damaged, and there were some big houses in front of those in Petyt Place and at one point I heard a weird sort of noise going on – somebody calling. I thought at first that it was a casualty trapped there, then I found that a policeman was going around and calling for casualties and making this weird sort of hallooing noise to see if anyone was there. All sorts of little things like that happened during the night. The other site of damage at the bottom of Danvers Street was very bad indeed and it didn't seem likely that anyone could be alive there, but some of the rescue party were working there, tunnelling into the debris to see if they could find anyone. The incident went on and there were certain technical things which one needn't repeat – connected with reinforcement of rescue parties, there was, for example, a lot of gas, town gas, coming out of the broken gas pipes, so that parties standing by were often overcome with that. There were little bits of salvage, rather pathetic little things that belonged to people, a workman's tools for example, gathered up, belonging to one of the people who was later on to be brought out of the debris dead, handbags, trinkets and so forth – these were all collected up, it was all part of our job to collect these things.

'Then suddenly somebody called

out: "There's another one coming!" and I remember looking up and seeing what I thought was another parachute mine coming down. It was absolutely terrifying. You couldn't look away from the thing and there you were, just trying to make yourself as small as possible in the debris, and I suddenly realised it wasn't a mine, it was a man, it was an airman on the end of this parachute, and he dropped down quite fast over the roadway and down on to the foreshore of the river, on the embankment. A number of us rushed across there and then we looked rather cautiously over the wall. We had ideas about paratroop invasions. I was clutching my axe and I expect everybody else was wondering what we could do if the man turned a gun on us, but someone went down the steps which are just a little way along the embankment there, and got hold of him. My recollection is that it was one of our wardens, called David Thomas, but anyway, he brought him up, and he was a youngster I should think in his early twenties. I remember he was wearing a green flying suit and he was pretty well the same colour himself. He was very correct in his behaviour – he didn't say anything, he didn't do anything, he just stood more or less at attention. I remember feeling his arm quite rigid when I got hold of him, and then something rather surprising happened – most of one's ideas were upset I think that night. Somebody rushed up and kicked him in the seat, very hard. I suppose it was somebody who'd had someone killed or was just overcome by the strain of events, but anyway he, the man who kicked him, then rushed round to the front of him and succeeded in getting a pistol out the pocket on his leg. He had a sort of pocket in front of his flying suit, and anyway, somebody else took the pistol from the little man, I don't know what he'd have done if he hadn't had it wrested away from him. Then a War Reserve policeman came along at that point, and shortly afterwards another one, and I remember seeing them marching this German airman off along the embankment, just as if he'd been drunk and disorderly on a Saturday night.'

And still the raid went on.

The great flares which hung as though fixed in the sky illuminated this little scene, the trees in Battersea Park and the rubble underfoot with equal brilliance. The throbbing of bombers and thudding of guns, the screaming fall and explosion of heavy bombs, the continual noise, had its own marked effect.

Incendiary bombs scattered over Post Don's area made spurts of fire all over the map. Fires were started in Paultons Square, Upper Cheyne Row, Danvers Street and Old Church Street. Mr Cremonesi's delicatessen store was on fire, but this was put out by a policeman, while he himself dealt with another fire at number twenty-five.

In every street there was a smell of bonfires and a sense of excitement. Women and elderly and unfit men vied with each other in lugging pails of water from one vantage point to another and pumping breathlessly until the flames were beaten down and they were left with their own small, charred, sodden victories.

Similar scenes were being enacted all over Chelsea (indeed all over London) and pins labelled 'H/E' were being steadily added to the Borough map at Control Centre to denote further major incidents. About four in the morning a parachute mine exploded on one corner of Chelsea Square, killing two firemen and a warden and injuring others. Another mine on Cranmer Court, just behind Chelsea Police Station, gave the German airman, who had baled out over the Old Church and who had been taken there, a considerable shaking.

And then all of a sudden it was quiet and the first sirens were sounding the All Clear in the distance. The sirens at the foot of Albert Bridge took it up and died away again. It was five to five. The raid had lasted seven hours and fifty minutes.

The heart of the City of London. The Bank of England on the left and the Royal Exchange in front, after a bomb had exploded in Bank underground station

The Cafe de Paris

On 8th March London had had its longest respite from bombs since the Blitz began, almost six weeks of raid-free nights, and in the Spring after the hectic days of the preceding autumn a normal life, or at least a normal wartime life, had been re-created; the theatres, shops, restaurants, pubs were functioning after a fashion. People did their jobs as best they could, and amused themselves as best they could, and thought of the morrow. The Blitz, in fact, even when it was first resumed in March, was already a thing of the past. The young officers who danced and died at the Café de Paris on 8th March were intended for other battles, in Africa, in Asia and in Europe. In a way that Saturday evening at the Coventry Street restaurant is comparable to the Duke of Brunswick's ball before Quatre Bras.

The Café de Paris is approached by a long flight of stairs, leading down from an inconspicuous entrance between the Rialto Cinema and the Lyon's Corner House in Coventry Street, Piccadilly. These stairs run down to a sort of foyer, off which are the cloakrooms, and which contains a bar. From the foyer or entrance hall the visitor steps out on to the balcony that circles the restaurant proper. From this balcony a double curved stairway leads down to the dance-floor, and between the stairs, at ground level, is the bandstand. Above the stairs and band, and facing the entrance hall, the balcony is deeper. Standing there, looking down at the dancers and diners below, one might almost imagine oneself upon the bridge of a ship, looking down upon the quarterdeck.

Since it was underground, the Café de Paris was believed to be safe. It was advertised as London's safest restaurant. This, however, was quite untrue. Above the restaurant are only two roofs, its own, and the roof of the cinema above that, for it is underneath the Rialto. The theory about the shelterers under the arches in Bermondsey applied to the rich as well: where they believed themselves to be safe they felt all right. And a powerful contributory factor to this sensation of safety, in Piccadilly as in Druid Street, was the absence of noise. In the Café de Paris it was not possible to hear the raids banging and roaring away outside. (And outside, of course, it was equally impossible to hear what was going on in that underground restaurant.) The Café de Paris, which had reopened during the height of the Blitz, rapidly became one of London's most popular restaurants. It was expensive, smart and gay. The big hotels, with their steady clientèle of rich, and therefore usually middle-aged, residents, lacked the appeal of youth of this most handsome, excellent and apparently safe restaurant, with its superb jazz – Ken Johnson, 'Snakehips', was there with his Caribbean band, undoubtedly London's best – its lovely décor, and its excellent food. For a young officer on leave, and not caring about the expense, the Café de Paris was the ideal place to take his wife or sweetheart.

Among those present on the evening of 8th March was Lady Betty Baldwin, the daughter of the former Prime Minister. Her war work was with the ambulance unit in Berkeley Square, and she was in charge of one shift, but that night her shift was off duty. She therefore decided to have an evening out, and went to the Café de Paris with three friends. She has told this writer that she remembers remarking on the quality of people who were there that evening – a thing, she says, which somehow she would not normally do. The men, almost all in uniform, seemed extraordinarily handsome, the young women very beautiful, the whole atmosphere one of great gaiety and of youthful charm. This was so striking that she could not forbear to comment on it, and it compensated for her moment of irritation at being unable to obtain her favourite banquette. The restaurant was crowded, and this banquette was taken. A little later all the people seated at that table were dead.

Though most of the diners had come to the restaurant by taxi, the homes of many were far away. Thus Lady Betty's escort was a Dutch officer. A Canadian convoy had recently docked at Liverpool, and a group of officers and nurses who had come to London that day were spending their first free evening on English soil at the Café de Paris. Mr Ulric Huggins, then an officer of the Royal Navy, had recently arrived from Bermuda and was dining with his newly married wife, a friend named Limbosch who was a Belgian army doctor, and the doctor's girl, an Austrian nurse. As already stated, the bandsmen were West Indians, the bartender an American, the waiters inevitably cosmopolitan. The star entertainer that week was Douglas Byng, but on the night in question he was performing at a big charity ball in Park Lane.

A very pretty English girl, now Mrs Trouncer, has said:

'Well, what I remember of this particular night is that we'd decided we'd dress up to go out. I can't think there was any particular reason for it, but I think that everybody was so worried and so gloomy that, you know, we thought we would. So I did have a dinner dress on – that I remember. And we went to one or two bars and we were feeling very gay and very happy and we went along, I suppose it was about half past nine, and as you say the place was very full, and everybody was very gay.'

Mrs Wittman, a most beautiful woman, has said:

'I should never have been there, had I taken my mother's warning, because she's very psychic and she had a dream a few days before, seeing me in her dream with my eyes bandaged and so on, and sent me a telegram begging me not to go. Anyhow, I had to go up for a regimental wedding and so we were all in town together, my husband and friends, and the Blitz was so bad we thought we'd like to get further underground. And the Café de Paris, having advertised so much how deep and safe it was, we thought that was the place. So they put a tin hat on my head and we walked and got to the Café de Paris where we felt much safer.'

A lady, Miss Irene Ballyn, has written:

'On the evening of Saturday, 8th March, I gave a small sherry party at our flat in Bayswater. As the evening wore on one of the party suggested going on to the Café de Paris to feed; Douglas Byng was billed to appear in the cabaret, and the friend in question was most anxious to hear him. Opinion was divided, but I was resolutely against the idea: was it premonition or not? I still wonder. Another suggested Quaglino's. Still undecided, we left in taxis.

'My friend who wished to go to the Café de Paris and I were in the same taxi, but the argument as to where we should go continued. The taxi-driver, warning us that it might well be a sticky night, implored us to make up

For those who could afford it, night life provided a welcome escape from the war, until the night clubs were hit

our minds. The alert was on, and when we reached Marble Arch we were confronted by a taxi upside down in the middle of the road and other signs of blast. At the sight of this the driver of our taxi said: "Now you've blooming well got to make up your minds. What's it to be – Café de Paris or Quaglino's?" My friend gained the day and we proceeded to the Café de Paris.'

Ken Johnson, known by the public but not by his friends as 'Snakehips', was exceptionally well-educated for a jazz-band leader, having among other degrees a musical doctorate. He was then sharing a house with Mr Gerald Hamilton, and, since he hurried over his dinner at the *Edu de France*, was a little earlier than usual in arriving at the Café de Paris. Mr Leslie Hutchinson, the trumpeter of the band and a close personal friend of Ken Johnson's remembers:

'Mr Ken Johnson came in in a hurry, and said: "Man, it's terrible outside – just terrible." '

Miss Ballyn arrived soon after nine o'clock:

'We were received by Charles, the head waiter, so much liked by all who knew him well. There was nothing servile about Charles, he was gracious, there was nothing patronizing about him, though he was friendly. The tables around the dance-floor were packed, but Charles could arrange for us a table on the balcony. Perhaps, said he, we would have a drink in the bar while waiting? So to the bar we went, and it was while we were there that it happened.'

Mrs Blair-Hickman, an extremely attractive Canadian girl, was there:

'It was just like a Canadian old home week, there were lots of Canadians, nurses, kilted officers, all sorts and types and sizes, and a lot of blue blood too, I gather. We got there only a few minutes I think before the bomb fell. We hadn't even ordered dinner. The boy I was with and I decided to dance, we went out on the floor, and the tune was *Oh Johnny!* ...'

Mrs Wittman had just sat down:

'We ordered our meal. We were sitting at the bottom of the stairs, and one of the men who was with us said: "How about dancing?" Paddy is a very good dancer, and I loved dancing, and yet after one round we stopped in front of the band, which was Snake-hips Johnson's, and I said: "Look, do you mind if we sit down? We've all night before us..."'

Ulric Huggins and his party were a few tables away:

'We arrived to the best of my memory round about a quarter past or twenty past nine. We took a table on the left of the dance-floor, underneath the balcony. There was a pillar between us and the main part of the dance-floor. We had a cocktail first and we'd been there some quarter of an hour or twenty minutes. We had ordered dinner, and ordered the wine. The waiter was standing behind me, pouring out the champagne over my shoulder for me to sample...'

Leslie Hutchinson says:

'Well, the band kept on playing, on and on, and Ken said: "Stop the band, and play *Oh Johnny!*" Of course we went to give *Oh Johnny!* and then about the second chorus I just heard like a *ping!*'

Mrs Wittman says:

'My first impression was that some-body had, for some reason, thrown a bottle in my face from the balcony, when I saw this blue flash, and every-thing in the air...'

Mrs Trouncer was on the floor:

'Fortunately on the outside of the dance-floor, quite happily dancing, and the next thing I would say I remembered was that I felt: well, this is the end of the world. It didn't really occur to me that it was a bomb. We'd been blown flat, you see; well, we got to our feet, and I remember turning round and seeing, well, my first sort of impression was that the light upstairs was on and therefore one got this extraordinary macabre sort of atmos-

phere, with all the dust and the bits of this and that, you know, and it looked rather like one's imagination of hell.'

Mrs Blair-Hickman:

'I always remember, it was like swimming through cotton wool, if you can imagine such a thing. I didn't lose consciousness, I don't think I could have done, I remember everything that happened, and when I sort of came to I was sitting on somebody, quite definitely sitting on somebody. It turned out to be an officer wearing a kilt. And I discovered that my leg was broken – I couldn't stand on it – and my back was very wet – that was blood, I found out later. I didn't feel anything at all except astonishment. We all expected in those days to be possibly bombed, but the actuality was so different, at least to what I'd expected. I looked around, there was a lot of dust, a lot of bodies lying around, and lights burning in the darkness.'

Miss Ballyn, it will be remembered, was near the bar:

'It is not easy to describe the actual moment. One had been in houses when it had happened nearby, and also in streets when houses had been hit, but this messenger of death fell among us. To the best of my recollection there I stood, with a glass in my hand, chatting. Then a sudden and very severe pressure on the top of my head. Then complete darkness. The next thing I knew, on opening my eyes, was that the place was in semi-darkness, the sound of groans, low cries, and whimpering. I was sitting on the floor, my back supported against the wall. A man was leaning over me, he had a glass in his hand. He told me to drink it, it was sal volatile.'

Mr Huggins, it will be recalled, had been sampling his champagne:

'The first impression I got was of darkness and dust, and I noticed the champagne bottle lying on the table horizontally. My first instinct at that moment was to pick up the champagne bottle and put it upright. It must have been a matter of some seconds afterwards that I remember I stood up, with the champagne bottle still in my hand, and poured out drinks for the other three people at the table. And a memory I have very clearly is that, as the champagne rose in the glasses, which incidentally were standing upright on the table unbroken, the foam on the top was grey with dust. And I remember quite clearly wiping the foam off with my finger before I drank. And then I turned round, and there at my feet was the waiter, who had been leaning over me pouring out the champagne – dead, of course.'

There were, in fact, two bombs that had fallen through the cinema and into the restaurant at approximately a quarter to ten. They weighed fifty kilos each. One exploded in front and just to the right of the band, at approximately chest height among the dancers, killing Ken Johnson,

A heavy raid in April 1941 that gutted the Holborn area

another member of his band, and thirty-two other people, and seriously wounding sixty more. The other bomb luckily did not explode, but burst assunder on impact with the dancefloor, scattering its stinking yellow contents over the dead and dying, and making a small hole in the parquet flooring: the pieces were later collected by a Bomb Disposal Unit. One of the two bombs had come down through the balcony, which was holed and sagging.

Most of the lights had gone out, but not all, for there was at least one burning on the balcony, casting a faint light among all the flying dust and debris. Somebody lit a cigarette-lighter and a stentorian voice shouted 'Don't do that! You'll blow the place up if there's gas about!' There was a pungent, acrid smell, the smell that is customary after a bomb or shell has exploded, and in this case perhaps reinforced by the pounds of high explosive scattered about when the other bomb was shattered. The glass mirrors had of course smashed into

thousands of murderous, flying stilettos. Mr Huggins' dead waiter had one small hole in his back, and had most likely been knifed by a glass dagger. Many people there have commented on the extraordinary silence, but this was probably because they were temporarily deafened. For others heard differently.

Mrs Goschen-Evans, for instance, became aware first of a sort of red Christmas-tree light, or a light with a red shade, burning above the bandstand. This must have been near where the head waiter and the manager had been standing, on the 'bridge' above the band, and where they had both been instantly killed. Then she became conscious of terrible screams close beside her. At first she thought that it must be herself screaming, and tried to stop, and it was only after a few seconds that she realised the screams were coming from a woman beside her. A bald-headed colonel was sitting on the stairs, which were half blocked with rubble shoulder-high, his head in his hands, groaning pitifully.

Down below there was horror. A girl had been celebrating her twenty-first birthday down there. Miss Ballyn says: '. . . . stripped of all her clothing by the blast, in fact stark naked, she was carried to me, covered with a tablecloth. She died while I was holding her.'

Mrs Blair-Hickman has said:

'A very large officer who I found later was Dutch, a lot of gold braid, peak cap, fully dressed with an overcoat as well (he probably came in off the street), picked me up and carried me through into the kitchens and laid me on the hot-plate, and he set my leg with a wooden stew-spoon, washing it first of all, believe it or not, in champagne, which was the only thing handy. While he was doing that a waiter, a very agitated waiter, was trying to clean off my face, which obviously was very dirty, with a napkin, and the awful thing about that was that my face was full of little bits of glass, it was absolute torture to have him do this. However, he was well meaning, and while he was doing that all round me on the floor there were casualties. There were a lot of Canadian nurses there that night and they were working like Trojans, really trying to help, and there was one boy who was right down beside me, he had an enormous wound in his back, a great big, gaping hole, and this nurse was trying to staunch it with a tablecloth. This boy, probably he was a little cock-eyed, he was saying – Well, it's not everybody who's been cut in on by the Luftwaffe – and then after that they started to improvise stretchers by using the screens, because the stretchers had run out or something, and I was carted up the rickety stairs and laid out in Leicester Square, and I remember lying in Leicester Square and just feeling that nothing mattered particularly, I wasn't in any particular pain, I just felt – dead – most odd.'

Miss Ballyn adds:

'There were by fortunate chance a number of doctors among the guests, and these took charge until the arrival of the first ambulance from Charing Cross Hospital. These doctors, working in the semi-darkness, were doing their utmost. The little first aid available soon ran out, and then underclothing was being torn up to make temporary bandages. Someone had found an electric point in the passage that had not fused. Flex was produced and the grim scene gradually came to light.'

It was very grim. Before the bomb fell, Mrs Trouncer had noticed a young airman, dining with his mother: 'A perfectly enchanting old lady and I mean he was obviously on leave. He was so sweet to her, and so kind and nice. And the next thing I remember was seeing this old lady completely dead, I mean her head was practically off her body, and the young man came at me and he said: "My mother's all right, she's all right, she's all right, isn't she?" And I said: "Oh yes, yes,

yes, she's all right." And I mean she was just as dead as she could possibly be, and I was feeling absolutely really numb in a way.'

Ulric Huggins, it will be recollected, had been dining with his young wife, a Belgian army doctor and a nurse. None of them was hurt at all, and they now set to work. He had described what they did in these words:

'Now Limbosch decided that he was going to act as a doctor in his true capacity here; our job was to bring the casualties, if any, towards this central point, where there was light and where the benches lent themselves obviously to the laying out of casualties. So the first thing to do was to clear a space round those, and we started moving the tables back from the benches, and stacking them on top of each other. We went to the next table and as we pulled it away so we found an elderly couple who had been sitting next to us. They were both dead – they'd been exposed apparently to the full direct impact of the blast – there was no visible sign of damage to them, but they were both stone dead. Rather peacefully so, if anything. So we moved them away and took the tablecloth off and just covered them up. I then told my wife, Pat, to go round and collect all the napkins she could, and then I started to go out onto the dance-floor myself. Well, now, the scene there was almost indescribable. I remember coming across a girl lying on her front, I think it was – yes, on her front, and she had a very bad wound in the back. I didn't know whether she was alive or dead, and so there was another man, I forget who he was, some other man in evening dress – I said: "Come and give me a hand with this girl", and we picked her up very gently and we took her across to the bench where Limbosch was wrapping his operations up, and we laid her out

there. She thought she was going to die and she had her left, I think, or right thumb blown off. She was in terrible pain.'

The girl in question, Miss Hylton-Simpson, has told this writer that her life was saved at the Café de Paris by the ministrations of Ulric Huggins and his friends. Mr Huggins goes on:

'I was carrying people in from the centre of the dance-floor and the whole of that part is a little confused to me, but I remember one extra-ordinary case, when I was somewhere out on the dance-floor and I found beside me a tall RAF officer, and he was wandering about rather vaguely, and suddenly I noticed that in his head there was a terrible hole, blood pouring out of it, a great deep hole in the left side of his head, and so I escorted him over to the bench and sat him down and left him there and what happened to him afterwards I don't know, but by that time people were rallying round the places where the lights were, so that they could do something about it. Napkins were being used to staunch the wounds, and about that period on one of my journeys to and from the bench I noticed something rather extra-ordinary.'

What he had noticed were some rather sinister figures who had arrived quickly on the scene. Mrs Blair-Hickman, it will be recalled, had been lying in a semi-coma across the corpse of a kilted officer. She has said: 'And then I saw somebody creeping around in a vague sort of dreamlike way, and this man came up, and he felt around. He felt my hand, which was lying relaxed – I really was feeling most odd – and I found, I realised later, that what he'd done was take a ring off my finger. He must have done that to quite a lot of other people.'

He had. And this is what Huggins had noticed:

'In amongst the people who were dead, amongst the tables bordering on the dance-floor, I noticed two men, both of whom were obviously not

people who would normally come to the Café de Paris, they had caps on their heads and they had sweat rags round their necks, and they looked scruffy and dirty and they were leaning down – I presumed, at that moment, helping, and I just paused for an instant and looked at those chaps – and do you know what they were doing? They were looting. They'd come down the back entrance, and I saw with my own eyes those fellows pick up a lady's handbag, whip through it and take out something I didn't see. They were just a bit further away from me and I couldn't see exactly what it was, and I went up to one of them and said – I think, as far as I remember – Get the hell out of here.'

Those squalid figures cannot have been at large in the Café de Paris for long. Others, including Mr Simons, who were quite conscious, saw no trace of the looters and a considerable number of handbags and gold cigarette-cases lost in the chaos were later returned to their owners or to their next-of-kin.

Where had they come from?

Such petty crooks tended, then as now, to hang about Piccadilly Circus where in wartime many deserters also congregated. It may have been such as these who slipped down the back stairs into the restaurant with the pretence of helping, but actually to steal.

Or it may have been the work of a more ambitious criminal organisa-

tion. Miss Hylton-Simpson, when in hospital as a result of her wounds suffered in the Café de Paris, found herself in the next bed to a girl who had also been wounded that evening by a bomb dropped in Soho. This girl was the proud mistress of a small-time gangster. She told Miss Hylton-Simpson that the gang which her paramour controlled specialised in looting. It had spotters out, who telephoned to the gang's headquarters news of any likely source of loot, such as a blitzed jeweller's. Her lover's men, she boasted, would often be on the spot even before the men of the civil defence. And it is possible that these were the men who stole the ring from Mrs Blair-Hickman's finger.

And in contrast with such baseness,

Pause for refreshment during a long night's firefighting in April

Miss Ballyn tells a story which surely counteracts the squalor and distaste of the, other.

An RAF officer had had the finger of one hand sliced off by flying glass. She led him to the ladies' cloakroom and was washing the stranger's hand under the cold tap. It was suddenly too much for her, and she started to cry. The officer said, simply: 'Don't cry, my dear. It's my hand, not yours.'

With the arrival, at long last, of the ambulances, these brave women and men who had done what they could for the others began, one by one, to depart.

An end to the bombing

When, towards dawn on 11th May 1941, the All Clear marked the end of yet another very heavy raid on London, few people can have guessed that the London Blitz was over. As it had begun, almost fortuitously and for another purpose, so it ended without any true climax, almost without any real ending, for there was to be one more heavy raid, on Birmingham, before May was out. But it was, in fact, over. On 22nd May Kesselring's Second Air Fleet moved its headquarters to Poznan. By early June its squadrons were also in the East and only Sperrle's Third Air Fleet, its bomber strength much depleted, was left in France and the Low Countries. On 22nd June the German armed forces attacked the Russians from the Arctic to the Black Sea.

Then it was clearly over, at least for the time being. But there was little reason to believe that this was more than a respite. The Red Army sagged and staggered backwards: as the Germans won victory after enormous victory, it began to seem unlikely

Mid-May 1941. The bewildered Londoners little realised it, but for them the Blitz was over. Hitler had turned his attentions against the Soviet Union

King George VI inspects a night fighter squadron at Middle Wallop, deep in rural England

that Russia would long be left in possession of any effective fighting force: and the Heinkels and Dorniers could, of course, be switched back to the west just as quickly as ever they had been moved eastwards. The civil defence services had to be kept up to strength and full efficiency.

It was to be almost three years before they were called upon again to deal with bombs in any significant quantity, and even so, when the little Blitz of early 1944 took place, the raids were pinpricks compared to what had gone before. But the men and women of the civil defence trained, and watched, and waited. Quite soon the public began to forget what these men and women had done for them. They were to hear, once again, accusations of wasting public money, of being nothing but a bunch of tea-drinkers and darts-players. The public, forgetful at the best of times, is doubly so in wartime, and perhaps many who complained about the wardens and firemen had not, in fact, been in London during the Blitz. The Communists, now that the fatherland of the proletariat was itself involved in the war, even claimed that it was they who had kept up the morale of London's masses during that terrible winter when their principal activity had been muted sabotage.

But all that lay in the future. On 11th May, as the firemen put out the night's fires, as the wardens and rescue parties dug for the buried, as the ambulances rushed the wounded and dying to hospitals and the mortuary vans collected the dead, as the housewives once again swept the glass from their door-steps and the dust and rubble from their floors, no Londoner could know that it was over. Twenty thousand Londoners never did know, for the bombs and the fires had sent them to sleep, for ever, in their London clay.

Across the road from Parliament,
Westminster Abbey was badly damaged
by incendiary bombs

Winston Churchill contemplates the bombed-out shell of his beloved House of Commons, May 1941

What had it proved, if anything, this first and fearful onslaught from the air on a great centre of population? It had proved Churchill correct, when he had said, nearly twenty-five years earlier, that the terrorisation of civilians was unlikely to win a war: a fact that the Allied bombings of Germany were to prove again before this war was over. And for us, living under the threat of infinitely worse aerial attack, this fact is perhaps significant. For those who would protest that no comparison between the Blitz and some future onslaught is possible, it may be replied that in October of 1940 the population of London expected that that great city would be wiped out just as surely, if more slowly, as we expect in the event of atomic war. But they looked the fear straight in the face and decided that the reality, horrible though it was, was neither so bad as the expectation had been, nor so repulsive as the alternative of surrender to a wicked and cruel enemy must be. Civilian morale did not crack then: there is no reason, despite hysterical publicists and strontium-mongers, to assume that it would crack again, even if conditions were far, far worse.

That is one lesson that may be learned from the Blitz. Another is the extraordinary adaptability, not always rational but nevertheless effective, of the inhabitants of a great city. Some people have talked, in the past, as though the bombing of London were a battle fought between the Londoners, particularly the civil defence services, and the Luftwaffe. This is not quite true. A fight in which one man stands defenceless while another punches him is scarcely a fight at all. But what is true is that the people of London displayed enormous ingenuity in dodging the punches as best they could, and enormous resilience in their ability to recover and to accept more punishment. Thus, though they in no sense 'defeated' the Luftwaffe, they frustrated Hitler's purpose, and that was a very real victory.

It was a tragic victory. London is not a beautiful city; with the notable exception of the Wren churches few of the streets and buildings that went had much architectural value. But the sentimental value of a home, whether it be designed by Nash or by some anonymous building contractor, remains, of course, enormous. And death can be measured against no scale. The death of young men in battle is shocking and tragic enough, though the generations of eternal war through which our ancestors have passed have made this tragedy seem, in the abstract at least and when it happens to others, almost normal. The death by violence of young women and of children is far more shocking, not only because we are even now not fully accustomed to such savage attacks on those who do not themselves kill, but also perhaps because such slaughter strikes at the very essence of our society and at its future. And when we look back across this half-a-generation, at the dead of that terrible winter, it is perhaps the women and the children whom we still mourn most vividly.

'During my time in the Fire Service,' Mr Phillips of Poplar has said, 'we had some bad times, we had some good times, some funny experiences and some tragic ones. But a sight that I don't think I'll forget ever was that of a rescue squad releasing a small child that had been buried in the collapse of a house. The child had been buried standing up, and was obviously dead. The rescue party were digging away, and they had just uncovered his head and shoulders. It was a terrible morning – rain was pelting down – and I can see now that child's head and shoulders, standing above the debris, white-faced and clean where the rain had splashed and washed the face of the child.'

Bibliography

War begins at home by T Harrison and C Madge (Chatto & Windus, London)
The Command of the air by Giulio Douhet (Faber & Faber, London)
Night Fighter by C W Rawnsley and Robert Wright (Collins, London. Ballantine Books, New York)
Hell came to London by Basil Woon (Peter Davies, London)
Post D by John Strachey (Gollancz, London)
Ack-Ack by Sir Frederick Pile (Harrap, London)
The Defence of the United Kingdom by Basil Collier (HMSO, London)
The Lesson of London by Richie Calder (Secher & Warburg, London)
Westminster in War by William Sansom (Faber & Faber, London)